Dagger
FIGHTING

CLEMENS NIMSCHOLZ
& RALF SCHOETZAU

Schiffer Publishing Ltd®
4880 Lower Valley Road • Atglen, PA 19310

Originally published as *Dolchfechten*:
Der mittelalterliche Kampf mit dem Dolch nach Meister Talhoffer
by Wieland Verlag GmbH, Bad Aibling, Germany
© 2012 by Wieland Verlag GmbH

Translated from the German by David Johnston

Library of Congress Control Number: 2015951249

Cover designed by Justin Watkinson
Type set in Arno Pro/Minion Pro

ISBN: 978-0-7643-4878-5
Printed in China

Published by Schiffer Publishing, Ltd.
4880 Lower Valley Road
Atglen, PA 19310
Phone: (610) 593-1777; Fax: (610) 593-2002
E-mail: Info@schifferbooks.com

For our complete selection of fine books on this and related subjects,
please visit our website at www.schifferbooks.com. You may also write for a free catalog.

This book may be purchased from the publisher. Please try your bookstore first.

We are always looking for people to write books on new and related subjects. If you have an idea for a book, please contact us at proposals@schifferbooks.com.

Schiffer Publishing's titles are available at special discounts for bulk purchases for sales promotions or premiums. Special editions, including personalized covers, corporate imprints, and excerpts can be created in large quantities for special needs. For more information, contact the publisher.

Contents

Foreword

If one thinks about medieval combat with edged weapons, then the long sword first comes to mind. It has characterized the image of the knight like no other and still emanates great fascination to this day. The long sword, which in some cases was wielded in two hands, was by no means the only weapon of the medieval fighter. There was also the short sword, which was often used with the buckler, a small shield. And another weapon was part of the equipment: the dagger.

Like combat with the sword, combat with the dagger was part of every fencer's standard program and was taught by the fencing masters of the Middles Ages with the same naturalness. The great teachers of the epoch, like Master Talhoffer, gave the same attention to the dagger as the longer weapons.

Clemens Nimscholz and Ralf Schoetzau have occupied themselves with medieval dagger fighting for many years. They have thoroughly researched the techniques—with an approach similar to that of experimental archaeology: they have studied and interpreted Talhoffer's writings before testing them in practice. They then used the results of these experiments to confirm or dismiss the respective interpretations.

This book is the result of years of work. It offers a comprehensive portrayal of dagger combat according to Talhoffer and, at the same time, is an historical reappraisal and a modern textbook. Each technique—is originating from the historical depiction in a manuscript—explained and illustrated is a series of photographs. In this way one can exactly reproduce the sequence of each technique.

I am convinced that the effort has borne fruit and resulted in a book that is truly unique. It makes its contribution to the state of modern medieval research and is undoubtedly a great help to present-day fighters who wish to complete their abilities.

Hans Joachim Wieland

From the Cod. icon. 394a

Chapter 1: Introduction

The rondel dagger and bullock dagger are not only weapons, they are also little beauties in a vast array of variations. There are single- and double-edged daggers, but also weapons with no edge at all with a three- or four-cornered blade. Mixed forms, with the upper part of the blade flat and only the tip—roughly the last ten centimeters of the blade—forming a triangle, are also known. To say nothing of the grips: many are examples of true artistry.

Equally as wonderful as the dagger itself, is the fact that there are still old manuscripts in which the use of the dagger is taught. These are fencing manuals that date from the Middle Ages and were written by fencing masters. These were men who, in addition to teaching their use, also used these weapons in combat. This allows us to assume that the techniques they taught worked and were also very efficient. Master Talhoffer, at least, lived to be very old.

The oldest of these fencing manuals dates from roughly the year 1300. Now known as the I.33, it resides in the Royal Armoury in Leeds, England. In the manuscript's handmade drawings a monk and his students demonstrate the use of the sword and buckler. Many old fencing manuals consist only of drawings, others have explanatory text in addition to pictures, and others consist entirely of text. But all of these combat manuals have one thing in common: they show more than simple strikes and thrusts. Instead they teach artistic handling with each class of weapon. In addition to thrusts and strikes, most also cover throws, levers and stopping techniques.

1.1 Practical Problems

Unfortunately it is not always easy to understand these instructions. Even if we have a picture illustrating the technique, it is usually no more than a snapshot, a fraction of a complex series of movements. We are then forced to reconstruct the technique's entire sequence of movements from this snapshot. Even if the illustration is accompanied by text, it does not always help. This is due in part because the language has changed greatly over the centuries and in part because the text is rarely of an explanatory nature and instead is often written in the form of short memory verses. For example, one will not find there: "If the attack comes, then go ...," instead simply, "For the upper thrust."

As far as language is concerned, much can still be easily understood, but much also cannot. And one must be careful when reading: at first glance many words seem to be familiar, but over time their meaning has changed.

Hans Talhoffer's Fechtbücher were written in the 15th Century and consists of drawings, some with brief accompanying texts. In this book we attempt to interpret Master Talhoffer's dagger techniques and represent them in a practical way. We realize that these are our own interpretations and that other fencers will probably come to different conclusions. But the techniques as we interpret them function demonstrably—which does not mean that we dispute that those of others do too. Apart from that, we also think that our interpretations reproduce what Master Talhoffer intended in his writings.

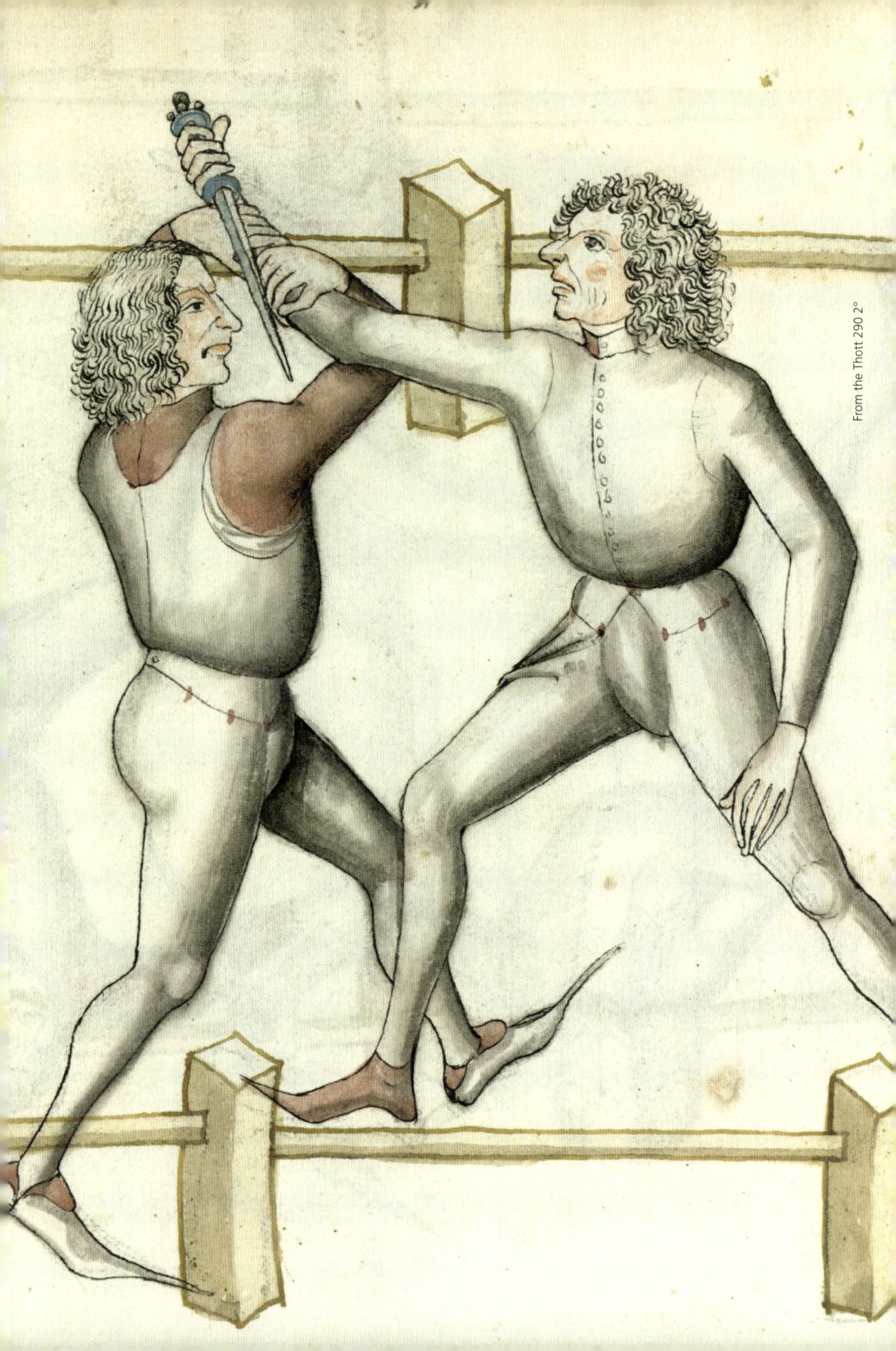

From the Thott 290 2°

We first tackled the illustrations and, if present, the associated texts, studying them and debating what they might mean. Then we assumed the positions shown in the drawings and conducted experiments to determine how one came to be there—rolling up the techniques from behind as it were.

After finding a path that led to the situations illustrated in Talhoffer's works, we checked to determine if the techniques also caused an effect. This means whether they broke an arm, caused severe pain, threw the opponent off balance or caused some other effect. Only if they showed such an effect, were practical, and equated to the drawings, were we content.

1.2 Sources

The materials available to us were manuscripts by Master Talhoffer or copies thereof: the Ms. Chart. A 558, the Thott 290 2°, the KK 5342, the Cod. Icon. 394a and the 78A15. In the beginning we thought that the works were by and large identical. But far from it! Of course, certain techniques that can be characterized as core techniques in the Master Talhoffer school of dagger fighting appear repeatedly in the manuscripts. But in every other manuscript that we saw there were additional techniques or details, resulting in a great overall diversity.

One exception is the 78A15. The techniques in it are the same as those in the KK 5342. We will therefore not also address this manuscript here.

Grasping the blade is seen quite often during execution of the techniques. On seeing this for the first time, one could think that Master Talhoffer had cut his fingers badly, but that is absolutely not so. For one thing, the daggers that Talhoffer used were not all sharpened. Daggers with a triangular or square profile with no edge were used in the Thott 290 2°, in the KK 5342 and in the Cod. Icon. 394a. They were pure stabbing weapons developed primarily for armored combat, for stabbing at small gaps in the armor.

Daggers with edges were only used in the Ms. Chart. A 558, although it is not clear how sharp these really were. Clemens, for example, possesses a replica of a rondel dagger. The blade is so sharp that one would have no difficulty cutting a cord with it. Nevertheless, one can grasp the blade without cutting oneself—provided one does it correctly!

Even sharp blades can be grasped with out gloves if one employs the proper technique. It is much less problematic with simple leather gloves, although understandably one must still be sure to employ the correct grasping technique. As a rule, of course, one should avoid grasping a sharp blade. On the other hand, in certain situations that can be the lesser evil. Cutting oneself is of course bad, but having a dagger thrust into one's body is much worse.

What surprised us at first is Master Talhoffer's recurring instruction to throw back the opponent; however, this gives him the opportunity to begin his attack again, this time perhaps with success. Thus it would actually make more sense to render the opponent *hors de combat* on the spot. Perhaps the reason is because that, in at least one of his manuscripts, Talhoffer gives instructions for trial by combat. In the Thott 290 2° we read:

> Thus whichever combatant comes out of the ring, before then the duel has its deadly ending, because he becomes knocked out of the ring by the other or he flees thereout, or however else he comes thereout; or he admits that the other man's challenge regarding the cause for challenge is right—then shall that man be adjudged vanquished …

Whoever left the marked-out combat area, whether voluntarily or involuntarily, had lost the battle. Which leads to the question: what did Master Talhoffer do if the opponent could not be defeated by leaving a defined combat area? Did he then push the opponent away from him or did he put him down on the spot?

Another interesting section of text from the Thott:

> Thus firstly you should know well the master who will teach you; that his art be right and protective; and that he be pious/sober; and that he not embezzle you; and that he not shorten/beguile the lore; and that he wits to broaden the arsenal wherewith he will battle. Should that master not accept that, swearing upon his profits ingratiatingly and his prejudices devotedly and thus shall his ilk become masters because of him—then swear neither ti further nor to teach his so-called art.

The essence of this section of text: the art must not simply be disseminated further. Could the reason for this be that the techniques in the manuscript are not explained more precisely? Were they intended merely as memorization aids for those who had learned the techniques, while one without training could do nothing with them?

Talhoffer's attention was not, however, directed solely at making his students fit and teaching them to use the weapon:

> Thus the master who has a student to teach, he shall wit that he recognize well the man whom he will teach: whether he be weak or strong and if he be coxcomb-raging or gentle-minded; whether he has good breathing/endurance or not; and whether he may work heartily...
>
> ...what be his nature? If he be strong or weak, if yet he be coxcomb-raging or not...

Master Talhoffer also looked closely at the nature of his student, in order to tailor the instruction to him and promote the student's positive qualities. But the nature of the opponent was also of interest: Talhoffer instructed his students on how to exploit the nature of his opponent to his own ends.

The fact that we often do not know from which situation the techniques are carried out does not exactly make their interpretation easier. It is not always clear who is the attacker and who is the defender. Is it always as it seems? The only exceptions are those illustrations that are accompanied by text, which explains who is the attacker. Are the fighters standing in a measure (a distance) in which they cannot reach each other before they move towards each other and execute the techniques? Or are the individual techniques snapshots from a combat or situations that occur during the "infight"? The relative positions of the combatants suggest that many techniques are indeed such situations.

Some attacks are carried out in such a way that the foot on the weapon-hand side is forward, giving the attack greater range. On the other hand, some attacks are carried out with the foot on the weapon-arm side not forward, which gives less range. One can now try to use this particular feature to distinguish between the attacks from a broad measure and those from the infight. Those with a long range are carried out from a broad measure. The attacks with a short range are executed from the infight.

Unfortunately that is not correct. It is equally possible that during an attack the weapon hand foot is not brought forward, in order to be able to effectively employ the other arm—which in dagger combat is entirely justified.

No matter whether the attacks are made from a broad or close measure: we have decided to undertake the reconstructions of the individual techniques from the guards. Thus a full step must always be taken to reach the opponent. This approach seems to us to be clearer and better suited to beginning practice.

The sequences of the individual "set-plays" (techniques) in the manuscripts are not necessarily step-by-step or structured logically. Thus displacements and guards, which one would expect to find at the beginning of a modern combat manual, are found here and there in most of Master Talhoffer's manuscripts. In the Cod. icon. 394a, one set-play is even arranged wrongly, with the counter appearing before the technique it is intended to address. It seems as if Master Talhoffer simply put to paper what was going through his head at the moment. In the process something as banal as structure apparently made no difference.

The various manuscripts also differ greatly in style. In Master Talhoffer's first work, the Ms. Chart. A 558, the drawings are still quite crude and the dagger section contains no supporting text. In some cases, it also appears as if the time window for executing the technique as represented in the drawings was very poorly chosen. Some drawings create the impression that often only the beginning or end of the technique is represented.

But, although many techniques are difficult or impossible for us to interpret, the Ms. Chart. A 558 is very interesting and full of tips. In one illustration one sees someone who, while falling, is stretching his leg toward the one still standing—a hint that one can still kick while falling? In another picture one is lying on the ground, the other is still standing. The one standing has placed his right foot on the shinbone of the man on the ground just below the knee. Is he doing this to control the man on the ground? Another illustration, which depicts one person lying on the ground and another standing, shows the former stabbing at the latter's thigh with his dagger. A hint that one should always be alert and must never underestimate the opponent, even if one believes that he has already been defeated.

On the other hand, the Thott 290 2° seems comparatively clear. The short notes and the naming of many techniques is pleasing. That is an advantage. Because it is always easier to speak about things that one can call by name. During training in particular it is simpler if one can name the techniques. The selected timings in the illustrations also seem to have been very well chosen. Combined with the text, they allow the techniques to be reconstructed quite well.

The techniques are also represented very clearly in the Cod. icon. 394a. Of course, here too one must ponder what is meant. Combined with the supporting texts, which are rather more substantial than those in the Thott 290 2° (although one cannot accuse Master Talhoffer of having used too much text), the techniques are relatively easy to reconstruct. In contrast to the Ms. Chart. 558, the timing of the technique illustrations is very well chosen, and the illustrations are of excellent quality. As with the Thott 290 2°, the illustrations in the Cod. icon. 394a alone make the manuscript a pleasure to look at.

The same is true of the 78A15 manuscript. At least as far as the dagger techniques are concerned, the KK 5342 is a copy of the 78A15. The techniques in it are depicted very clearly. The artist has succeeded very well in capturing the body dynamics. Here, too, the supporting text is very helpful.

As our book is intended to be both a reconstruction and an introduction to training, we have tried to arrange it in a logical sequence. A brief introduction to the history and sources is followed by the individual techniques that are thematically arranged, beginning with the basics, and simple, fundamental techniques. Each technique is illustrated step-by-step in photo sequences—just as one would expect in a modern textbook.

1.3 No Sport

In the Asian fighting system a differentiation is made between combat sport and the martial arts. Put simply, combat sport was developed in the late Middle Ages in order to allow the warrior to pursue his usual activities without injuring anyone. Modern combat sport is designed so that the possibility of injury is minimized, which means that it is strongly curtailed. For example, many techniques simply cannot be practiced in competitions if one wishes to preclude serious injuries or worse.

The martial arts, on the other hand, strive to be a real fighting system with no limitations. This makes a true free fight impossible if serious injuries and death are to be avoided.

Historical fighting is a mixed form of both styles. It tries to come as close to reality as possible, in that the combatants are protected against blows from dull weapons by wearing protective clothing. This makes a full-contact free fight possible, in which throws and some levers are possible with caution. Here too, of course, there are techniques that are forbidden, in order to avoid serious injury.

The combat manuals of the old masters in general and of Master Talhoffer in particular come from a time in which the fighting art was not only practiced for sporting purposes. It was really used in life-and-death combats—whether in dark alleys at night, during feuds, in war, in trials by combat or wherever. As playful as they might sometimes seem today, the fencing manuals were anything but a series of sporting exercises. They were a guide on how to kill an opponent, in order to survive.

But they are even more than that: they are our cultural legacy. What the oriental fighting system is to the Asians, historical fighting is to us Europeans. It is an art that was developed by our forefathers' generations hundreds of years before. And just as the Asians are justifiably proud of their heritage, so should we be proud of ours. We therefore consider the reanimation of the old fighting arts a rediscovery of part of our culture.

In our modern usage, the term fencing is restricted to familiar fencing weapons like the foil, dagger or saber. For the old masters, however, fencing was much more than that. There was fencing with the sword and buckler, fencing with the long sword, fencing with the dagger and much more.

If we seriously want to pursue fencing with the dagger, then we should come as close as possible to what the masters wanted to convey in their manuscripts. We should never allow it to degenerate into a gym lesson or a recreational sport with elegant exercises. Instead we should try to preserve as much of this effective fighting system as possible with as little adulteration as possible.

Of course, if we wish to carry out a free fight, we must regulate what is permitted and what is not. But at least we can again incorporate the omitted techniques in our technique training. One can then argue that in the heat of battle in a free fight it is difficult to avoid using techniques that have been practiced. That is true. But it we omit them entirely, then we begin to curtail our system and forget elements of it and we inevitably make a martial art into a fencing sport.

In a serious fight one does not care about sportsmanship or fairness, rather the objective is to get out of the situation as intact as possible. The most intelligent thing to do is run away, if that is possible. If it is not, then we do everything possible to save our skin, including, if necessary, scratching, spitting and biting.

This is also what the old master fencers did. While there is no evidence to prove that they scratched, spat or bit, there is proof of other things that were less than sporting. There is a picture in Talhoffer's fencing manual in which one of the combatants is kicking the other in the knee. According to the accompanying text, the object of this was to break the knee. In Plate 45 of the KK 5342 a fencer strikes his opponent in the face with his fist. Another illustration in the Thott 290 2° shows a man poking his opponent in the eyes to break his grip. In the Libr. Pict. A 83[1], an illustration shows one combatant kicking the other in the privates with his foot and kneeing him in the abdomen. He also pulls on the other's beard.

In another illustration (see page 174) the fighter on the left first throws his hat in his opponent's face to temporarily blind him and then throws his dagger at his chest. Unfair? Possibly. But what counted in the end was that he won the fight and went home again.

But what use to us is this knowledge of dagger fighting? It makes us aware that the entire opponent poses a threat, not just his dagger. We must expect anything at any time and always be on guard. Even

From the Cod. icon. 394a

Unrefined but effective technique: here the opponent is kicked in the knee.

if we have firmly grasped the opponent's dagger arm, we must always be ready for a blow, kick, head butt, throw, lever or something else with which the opponent will defend himself as best he can. If one has grasped the opponent's dagger arm, one must pay particular attention to his free arm and free leg. The free leg is the one that carries most of the body weight. Sometimes it is also both legs.

1.4 Conventions

At the end of the introduction a few words about the parlance used in this book. In dagger fighting there are two ways of holding the dagger. For lack of a better term we will use the following: grasp the dagger short or long.

[1]Anonymous: Berlin State Library, Prussian Cultural Holdings, Libr. Pict. A 83. Southern Germany, possibly Nuremberg, first quarter of the 16th Century.

We call the grip in the picture above, holding the dagger short, while the one in the picture below is holding the dagger long.

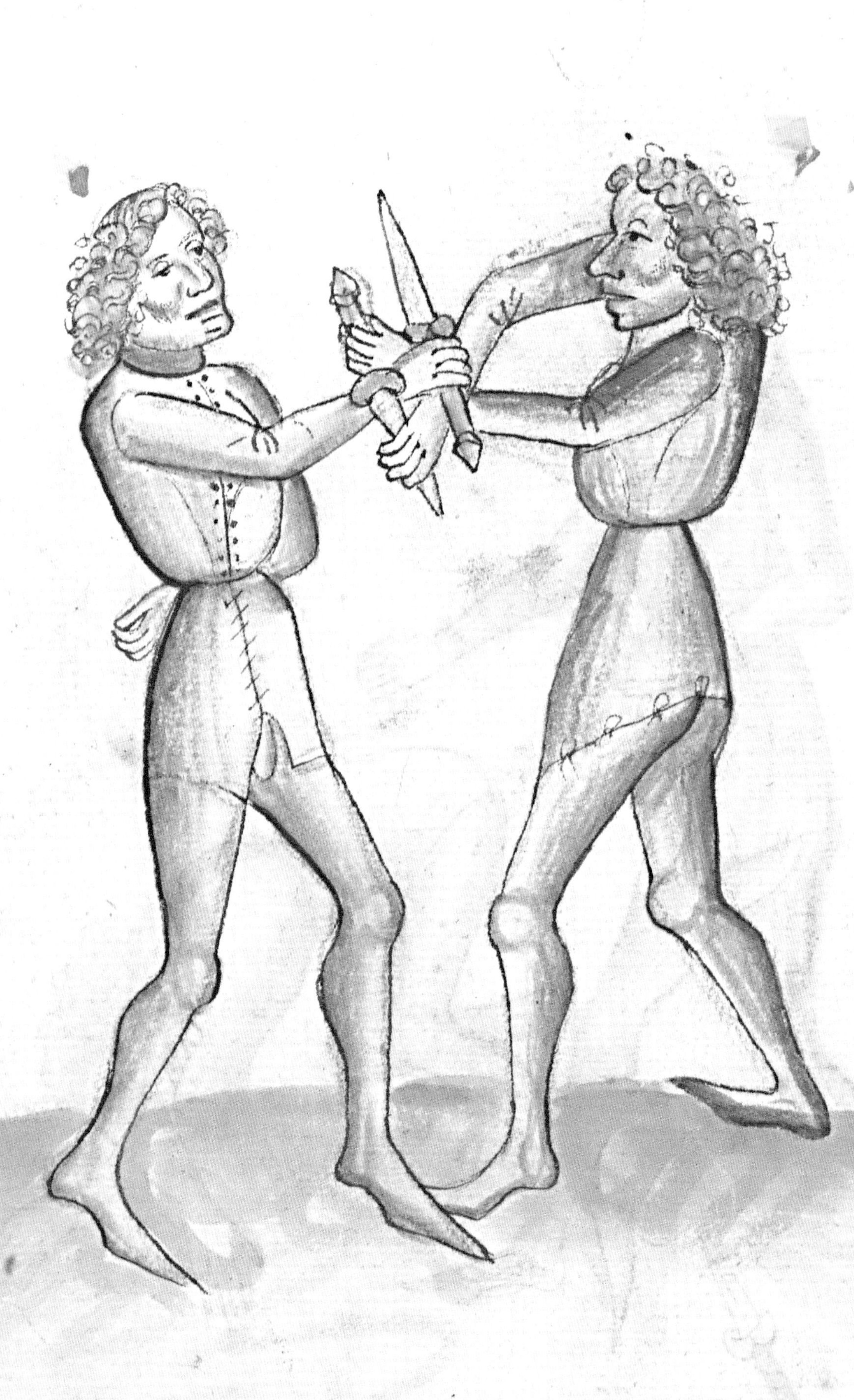

From the Ms. Chart. A 558

Chapter 2:
The Dagger

The principal weapon found in the old fencing manuals is the *Scheibendolch*, or Rondel Dagger, but the so-called *Nierendolch*, or Bollock Dagger, is sometimes also seen. Master Talhoffer mainly used the rondel dagger, and the bollock dagger is only seen in the Chart. A 558.

The rondel dagger spread across large parts of Europe from the 14th to 16th Centuries. There were many versions with different blades, grips and sizes. Some blades had a triangular or rectangular profile. These were used mainly in armored combat but also in trials by combat. A thin squared blade was more suitable for this than a normal flat knife blade. Because of its smaller profile, it was easier to thrust into small gaps in the opponent's armor. As well, such a blade did not break as easily as a flat blade if one mistakenly struck the armor and not the gap one was aiming at.

The rondel dagger was carried mainly by knights and nobles, but also by wealthy citizens and—as may be derived from some illustrations in old manuscripts—in some cases also by craftspeople. Short rondel daggers had a blade length of about 17 centimeters, while larger ones had blades up to about 40 centimeters in length.

In the Thott 290 2°, Master Talhoffer left us a short verse in addition to a drawing of a rondel dagger:

> This dagger should have a blade four hands long or more. Fight with the dagger in the right hand and the swiveling buckler in the left hand.

In quotations by Talhoffer one often encounters the word "Tegen." That was the word for dagger in Talhoffer's day.

The bollock dagger was common across large parts of Europe from the early 14th Century to the 18th Century. It was often worn on the front of the belt as a phallic symbol. This type of dagger was usually called kidney dagger in Germany but was known as the bollock dagger in England. It also came in many different variations. There were no limits to the shape of the grip, as long as the "balls" were still apparent to some degree. The same was true of the rondel dagger's blade. There are also

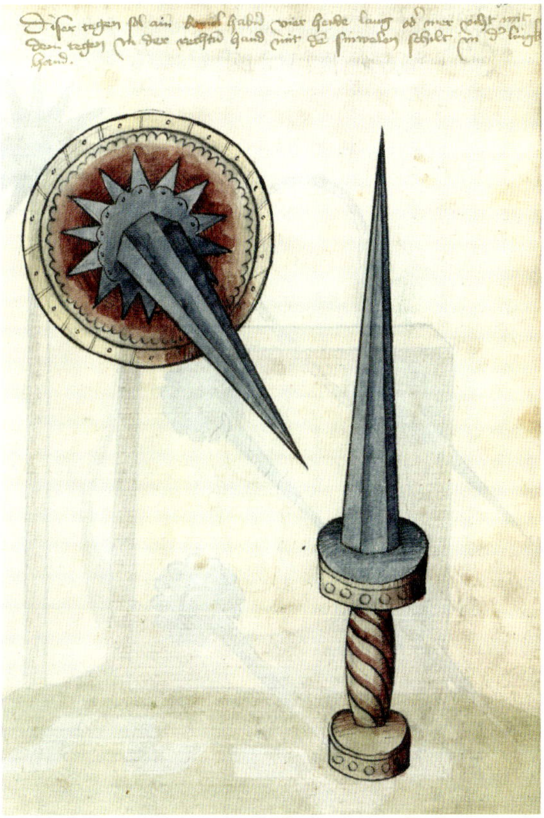

From the Thott 290 2°

surviving examples of mixed forms between the rondel and bollock daggers. The weapons smiths of the Middle Ages were extremely creative and constantly tried to produced new compositions.

Like the rondel dagger, there were bollock daggers with squared, single-edged and double-edged blades. Some examples were almost 50 centimeters long. Most bollock daggers had a metal plate at the end of the grip. The ones used in the Ms. Chart. A 558, however, were quite unusual, because the end of the grip was shaped like the head of a penis.

Left a bollock dagger from England, made in 1450. A brass trademark is inlaid in the blade. On the right, is a rondel dagger from Germany (15th Century).
Photo: Lutz Hoffmeister, German Blade Museum, Solingen.

2.1 The Practice Dagger

In general we do not use sharp daggers in practice. A practice dagger made of wood is used instead. One can purchase them already made or fashion them oneself. As Ralf enjoys making them, we use homemade practice daggers. We have chosen a relatively long dagger. In principle, however, one can use a simple stick for the first dagger practice. We have used cooking spoons or a rolled-up newspaper. Whatever you use, be sure that it is not too pointed! A ball at the tip of the blade prevents stabbing injuries. The wooden practice dagger has a ball on its tip.

One actually needs two different practice daggers: one with a stiff blade, so as to be able to practice the lever with it, and one with a flexible blade which yields when a stab is made. One can then stab in a free fight without causing injuries to the training partner. Unfortunately, to our knowledge there are no training daggers that combine both features.

If one already has several daggers, one of them should have a blade with three or four edges like many of the historical, bladeless daggers have. The lever techniques, such as the Islet for example, take on an entirely new quality if executed with a sharp blade.

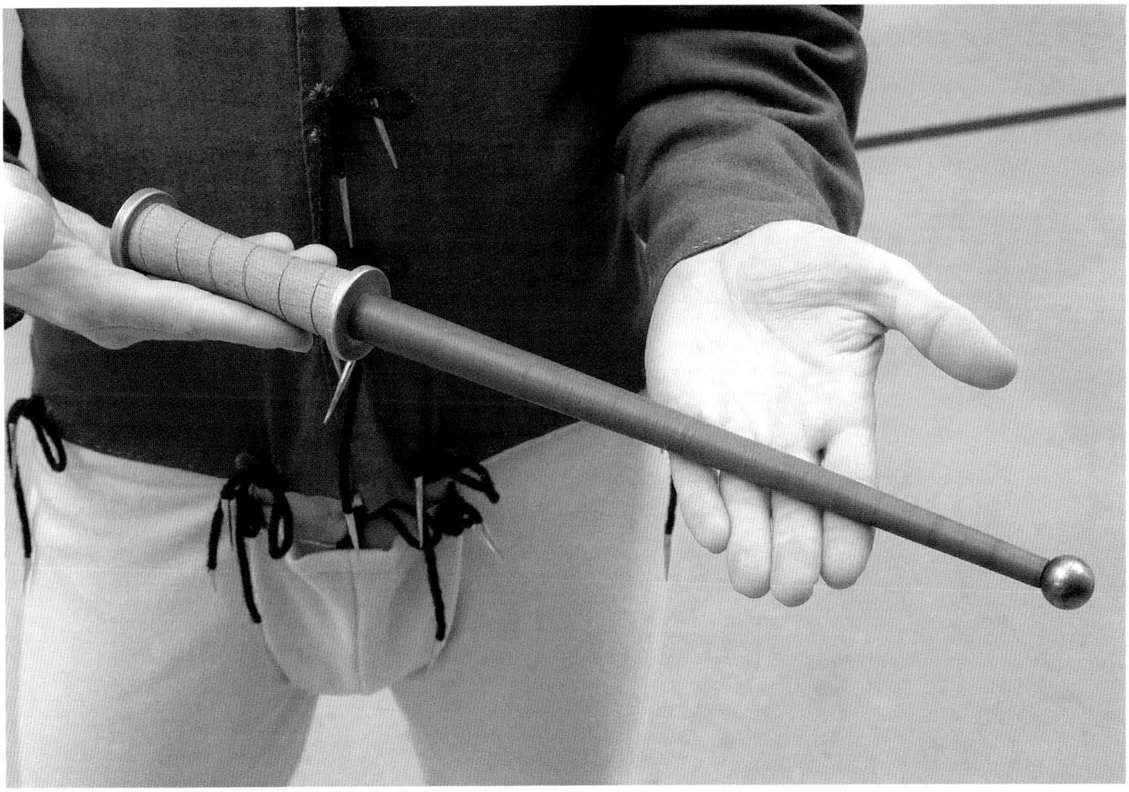

A harmless, homemade practice dagger with a ball at the tip that prevents injuries.

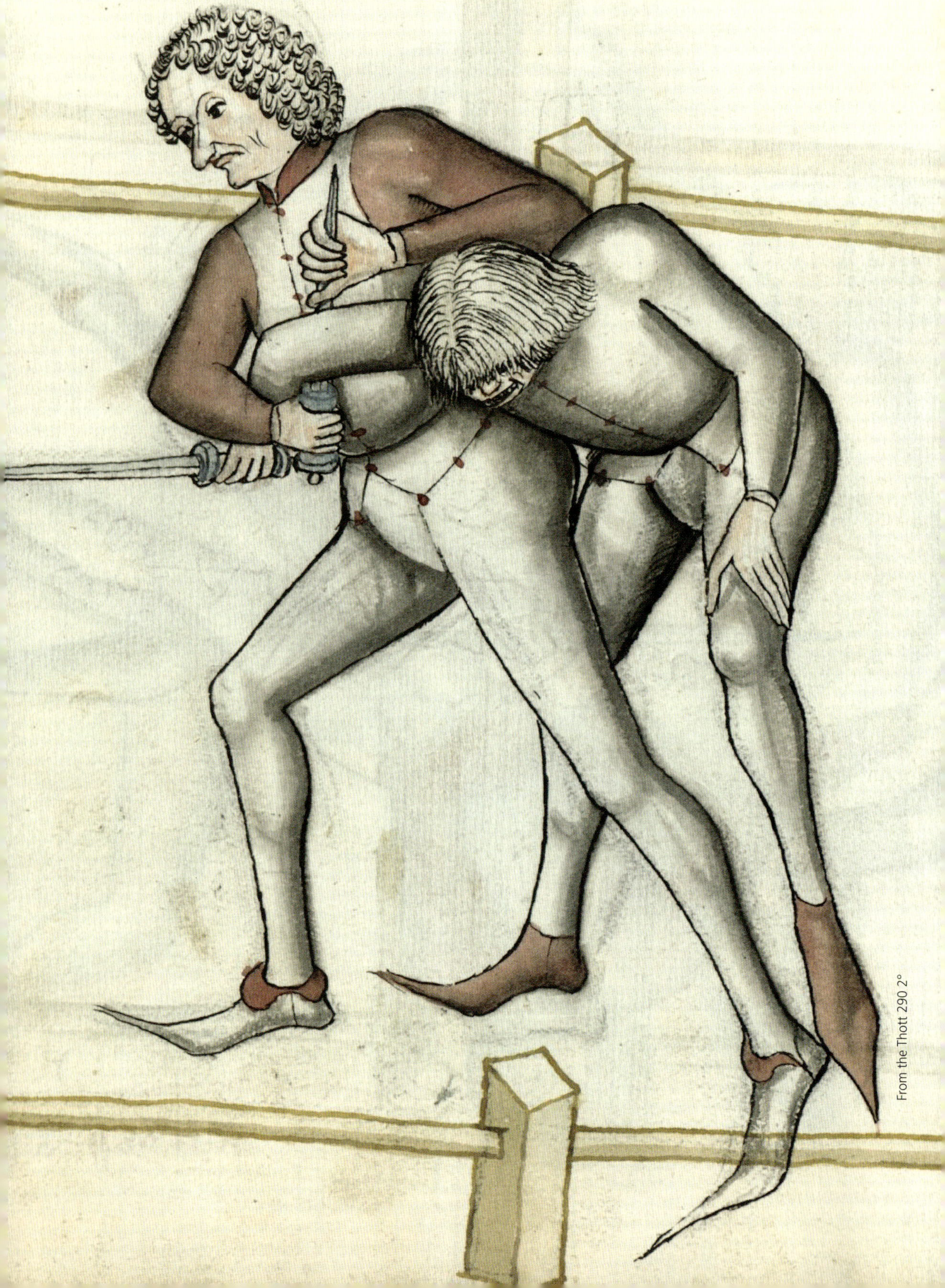

From the Thott 290 2°

Chapter 3: Master Hans Talhoffer

Hans Talhoffer was a German fencing master of the Middle Ages and probably the best-known fencing master of his day. He lived from 1423 to 1497—quite a long time for a man who made his living from the weapons trade. Apart from that he had a very long lifespan for the period in which he lived. Master Talhoffer taught combat and also wrote a number of manuscripts. His area of specialty was trial by combat. He could be engaged as an instructor, in order to be prepared by him for trail by combat. His manuscripts speak of this. Once he even stood in the ring before judges as a substitute combatant.

He probably resided in Franconia at the start of his career. In 1454 Master Talhoffer was in Zurich, where he taught fencing in the local town hall. The Zurich statute books from that year tell of this. It is recorded that, as per "school law," Master Talhoffer was present at a combat between two residents of Zurich. In his capacity as a fencing instructor he "intervened," whereupon one of the combatants went after Master Talhoffer with his sword (how irrational).

It is also known that he was a member of a brotherhood of fencing masters which was very popular at the time: the Brotherhood of the Virgin Mary and of the Holy and Warlike Heavenly Prince Mark, known as the *Marxbrüder* or Marx Brothers.[1] In the Thott 290 2°, Talhoffer delved into the rules of single combat:

> Thus he who was challenged, he comes singularly before the three tribunes to respond and gainsay. Therefore the man who was challenged, he speaks thus that he be blameless and he repeats that the accusations be not true and thereover he would honor with struggle upon that knowledge, as then be right for and required by the land wherein this be and so thereupon is dealt his training time. So he is dealt six weeks and four days from this tribunal for his training time. Thereupon is also dealt that the men shall struggle as is customary and right in the land...

Master Talhoffer then came into play in his capacity as a teacher. As previously mentioned, it was possible to hire him to prepare one for combat. The Swabian knight Leuthold von Königsegg did just this and took Master Talhoffer into his service. The KK 5342 tells of this occurrence.

A number of Master Talhoffer's fencing manuals have survived to the present day. In them he teaches the use of the long sword, armored combat with spear and sword, the Lucerne hammer, cudgel and shield, combat with the dagger, combat with the sword and buckler, wrestling, the long knife, trial by combat and more. Talhoffer also describes all sorts of curious fighting equipment, including a diving suit. He also touches on astronomy, anatomy and several other subjects in his writings. In total, nine works by Master Talhoffer on the art of fencing have survived, but only six of these were completed while he was alive. The other three are copies from the 16th Century.

WORKS WRITTEN DURING HIS LIFE:

Gothar, Gothaer Forschungsbibliothek, Ms. Chart. A 558 (subsequently called Ms. Chart. A 558), the oldest of his works. It is dated to 1443 and today resides in the Research Library in Gotha. It consists of 150 pages and contains 165 watercolor and washed pen drawings plus 15 black-and-white drawings. It is written in the Bavarian-Franconian vernacular. The manuscript contains the note "*yhesus Xps amen. 1443*," which indicates that it was begun after 1443. The text "*Hye hebt sich an meister liechtenauers chunst desz langen swerts anno domini xlviii jar*" could suggest that the book underwent a long production process and was not completed until the year 1448. It can, however, also refer to an original from 1438. Hidden under glue and chalk was a clue to its first owner, who was probably Master Talhoffer himself: The "*buch ist maister hannsen talh.*" The rest was unfortunately destroyed by worm damage.

Königseggwald, Bibliothek Königseggwald, Hs. XIX 17-3, is dated between 1446 and 1459 and today resides in the Count's Library in Königseggwald. It consists of 61 pages, has 111 color drawings and is written in the Swabian vernacular. It is a commissioned work that Master Talhoffer completed for the nobleman Leutold von Königseggwald. Master Talhoffer prepared Junker Leutold for a trial by combat which he had to contest. Part of the book therefore dealt with this single combat.

Berlin, Kupferstich-Kabinett der Stiftung Preußischer Kulturbesitz, 78A15 (hereafter referred to as 78A15) is dated to 1459 and currently resides in the Copper Plate Engraving Cabinet of the Foundation for Prussian Culture in Berlin. It consists of 78 pages, has 142 color pen-and-ink drawings and is written in the Swabian vernacular. According to a text that reads "*da stat her dauid und buppelin vom stain gebrueder vnd hand die kunst duy in diesem büch stat gelernnet von Hansen dalhofer*," the book was most likely a commissioned work which Talhoffer produced for the brothers David and Buppelin von Stain zum Rechtenstain.

Kopenhagen, Königliche Bibliothek, Thott 290 2° Alte Armatur und Ringkunst (hereafter referred to as Thott 290 2°) is dated to 1459 and currently resides in the Royal Library in Copenhagen. It consists of 150 pages, contains 257 watercolor drawings and is written in the Swabian vernacular. Its first owner was Master Talhoffer himself. According to a text passage, Master Talhoffer and his assistants posed as models for the drawings:

> *In the year of our Lord 1459: thus this book is that of Master Hans Talhoffer; and he is self-avowed with his life that someone has illustrated this book according to him; and that it became illustrated during Pentecost in that year after the birth of our beloved Lord Christ which is the one-thousand-four-hundred-fifty-ninth year thereafter. Truly, Michel Rotwyler scribed "me" the book.*

München, Bayerische Staatsbibliothek, Cod. icon. 349a (hereafter referred to as Cod. icon. 394a), is dated to 1467 and currently resides in the Bavarian State Library in Munich. It consists of 137 pages, which have 331 watercolors and washed pen drawings, and is written in the Swabian vernacular. The coat of arms shown on Page 16v (r "recto" stands for the front side, v "verso" for the reverse side of each page) suggest that the manuscript was a commissioned work that Talhoffer completed for Count Eberhard Im Bart of Wurttemberg.

PROBABLY COMPLETED AFTER TALHOFFER'S DEATH:

Wien, Kunsthistorisches Museum, Hofjagd und Rüstkammer KK 5342 (hereafter referred to as KK 5342), (formerly P 5342B; before that *Cod. Ambras*

55), made between 1480 and 1500. The book currently resides in the Art History Museum in Vienna, Collection of Historical Arms and Armour. It consists of 66 pages with more than 108 watercolors and washed pen drawings and is written in the Swabian vernacular. The identity of the customer and first owner is not known. The KK 5342 is an incomplete copy of the Hs. XIX 17-3.

COPIES FROM THE 16TH CENTURY:

Augsburg, Universitätsbibliothek, Oettingen-Wallerstein Cod. 1.6.2° I, produced between 1555 and 1560. It currently resides in the University Library in Augsburg. The Oettingen-Wallerstein consists of 67 pages with 112 washed pen drawings and is written in the Swabian vernacular. It is an exact copy of the HS XIX. 17-3.

Privately Owned, Cod. Ser. Nov. 2978, produced in the 16h Century. It is currently privately owned. It consists of 278 pages with 268 washed pen and colored drawings and is written in the Swabian vernacular. It is a copy of the Cod. icon. 394a.

Solothurn, Solothurner Zentralbibliothek, Solothurn S 554, produced between 1506 and 1515. Currently in the Central Library in Solothurn. It consists of 32 pages and has 57 watercolor pen-and-ink drawings without text. It is a fencing and wrestling book which illustrates set-plays with the techniques of Master Talhoffer. It is apparently not a copy of a manuscript by Master Talhoffer himself, however.

Because we could only see the Ms. Chart A 558, the Thott 290 2°, the KK 5342, the 78A15 and the Cod. icon. 394a, we also only cover the dagger techniques from these works in this book. We will not deal separately with the 78A15, as the dagger techniques it contains are the same as those in the KK 5342.

Professor Matthias Johannes Bauer (Professor of German Literature and Linguistic History of the Middle Ages and the Early Modern Era at the Technical University in Chemnitz) graciously alerted us to the fact that the formulations used often in the book, such as "Master Talhoffer wrote" or "Master Talhoffer shows" are wrong or at least doubtful. The statement "Master Talhoffer wrote" is definitely wrong, as Talhoffer did not write the manuscripts himself, instead engaging scribes to do the job.

Concerning the techniques, it has not been definitively proved if they were executed by Master Talhoffer exactly as they are depicted, or whether the artist allowed himself to be affected by outside influences or changed something. We would find that very surprising however, as it is difficult to imagine that Master Talhoffer would not discuss the contents with the scribes and illustrators and check their work.

The wordings "is found in the manuscript" or "according to the manuscript" would therefore be factually correct. However, as we assume that the texts and illustrations contain the teachings of Master Talhoffer, impart his knowledge and thus illustrate his techniques and reproduce his words, we adhere to the chosen formulations.

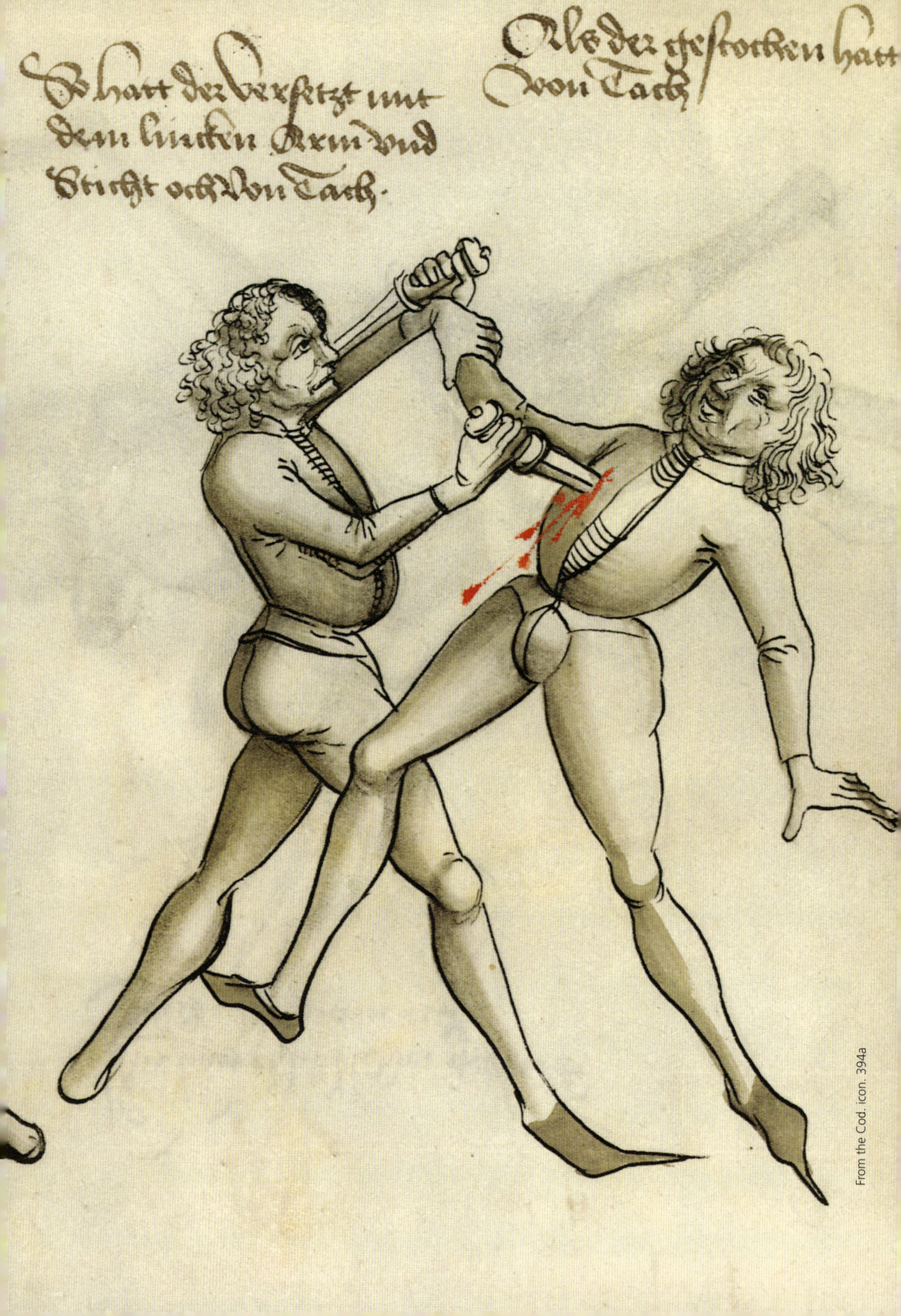

From the Cod. icon. 394a

Chapter 4: Basic Techniques

We now begin with the fundamental techniques. These will be followed by the complex sequences that consist of attack, defense and counterattack. We have given each technique a name—simple ones, for the reason that only they can permit a reasonable practice. One must be able to identify a technique in order to be able to practice it with another. Descriptions such as "the technique in which one does this above and this below" are not really helpful.

Several of the techniques have already been named in the historical manuscripts. In some cases the names were even the same in the different manuscripts, which is by no means a matter of course. Some techniques were called by one name in one manuscript and by another in a different manuscript. It also happens that some techniques are illustrated in different stages of the technique sequence in the different manuscripts. This can easily lead to confusion.

Of course, we have retained the names of those techniques that were clearly named. For those techniques with several names, we have decided on names that seem more descriptive or at least create as few conflicts as possible with the other names. Where techniques have no obvious name, we have tried to select something suitable from the accompanying text (where such exists). Only in a very few cases did we really have to come up with a new name.

In each case, we also show the manuscript in which the technique is to be found. In the case of techniques that are found in more than one manuscript, we have limited ourselves to one source. The relevant page of the manuscript is illustrated, so that the reader can always compare the historical original and our interpretation.

The structure of this book follows the rising complexity of the contents: the guards, displacements and thrusts are followed by the techniques themselves. We have divided these into three themes: after the pure counter-thrusts follow the techniques in which an unarmed fighter faces an opponent with a dagger, then the techniques in which both combatants have a dagger. The last two groups also include the use of levers, throws and similar techniques.

We—the two authors—appear in the photos. The combatant with the light top is Clemens Nimscholz, the one with the dark top is Ralf Schoetzau. To simplify descriptions of the photo sequences, hereafter the two actors are called Clemens and Ralf.

4.1 The Guards

As in all the other fencing arts, dagger fencing includes guards. What is a guard? It is a position in which one awaits the opponent's attack, a posture from which one can start attacking the opponent. This answer is incomplete, however. Guards are also situations that arise in combat. There are postures or movements with which one can defend against an opponent's attack or break through or circumvent his defense. There are snapshots of body position that begin or end an action of a certain kind. One should always be aware that guards are more than just positions, as they are essential in combat. One should therefore pay them appropriate attention.

If one assumes a guard at the beginning of a fight, one does so to counter what the opponent's body position suggests he is about to do. In every guard the front foot and thus the front knee points toward the opponent, which is also important. If we do not have the front knee aimed straight at the opponent, it is possible to twist and injure the knee when moving forward. The proper position takes some getting used to, but after a while it feels quite natural.

At the end of this chapter (pages 35 and 36) there are two guards from the KK 5342 in which the fighters have no weapons. They come from part of the manuscript that deals with wrestling. We have nevertheless included them, for we feel them relevant for the set-plays dealing with unarmed combat against an opponent with a dagger. Unfortunately these guards are unnamed in the KK 5342. All that appears there is "The beginning in wrestling." As the body posture is rather closed in one instance and very open in the other, to differentiate we named them "The beginning in wrestling, open" and "The beginning in wrestling, closed."

VOM DACH (From the Roof)

From the Cod. icon. 394a

"Der wyl obnen Nyder Stechen"

The From the Roof guard is intended for the thrust from above. Most of the attacks in Master Talhoffer's manuscripts come from it. It is, however, shown with different body positions in the various manuscripts. Once the posture is shown as leaning forward slightly (KK 5342), once very extended (Cod. icon. 394a) and another time with the arm clearly extended backward (Thott 290 2°). The Ms. Chart. A558 even contains a From the Roof guard with the dagger held long.

The stance is usually upright, the right arm held up and back, with the dagger held short with the point facing the opponent and the tip of the blade pointed at the opponent's face. The opponent should perceive our dagger to be a permanent threat. The stance is somewhat more than shoulder wide, and the knees are bent slightly. The front foot faces the opponent, the rear points forward at an angle of about 45 degrees.

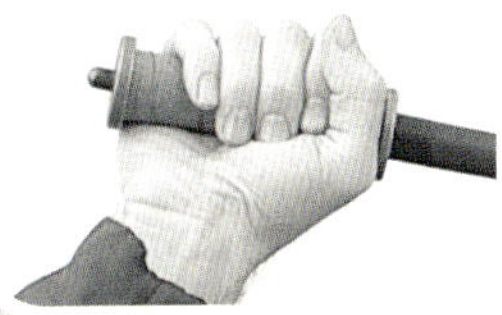

In the small photo above, the variation of the From the Roof guard with the dagger held long.

DER EBICH (The Ebich)

From the Cod. icon. 394a

"So gatt der unden uff mit versatzung und syls im Brechen"

In Master Talhoffer's manuscripts, the Ebich is associated exclusively with the defender. No attacks are shown from it, nor does any attack look to some degree as if it came from this direction. The Ebich is a guard that is used very frequently when the combatant is threatened with an attack from the From the Roof Guard. In the Cod. icon. 394a, therefore, it is only referred to as a break (counter-technique) for the From the Roof Guard.

The Ebich is depicted in the various illustrations with only minimal variations. The stance is quite wide and deep. The front foot points in the direction of the opponent, the back foot to the rear at an angle of about 45 degrees. In this stance, the weight rests somewhat more on the back leg. The right shoulder faces forward, and the upper body is turned to the side. The dagger is held short, close to the body, just above the groin, with the tip toward the opponent.

DIE UNTERE HUT (The Lower Guard)

For the KK 5342

"Der stat in der undern hut In den dritten stich"

The Lower Guard is found only in the KK 5342 and the 78A15. The depictions are identical, which is not surprising because the dagger is identical in both manuscripts. In the Lower Guard, the left foot is forward, the knees are slightly bent, the front foot faces forward, the rear foot points forward at an angle of about 45 degrees. The stance is somewhat more than shoulder-wide, and the weight rests mainly on the front foot. The rear leg is kept under tension, ready to rush forward. The dagger is held horizontally at the hip level, with the point toward the opponent. The left hand rests on the left thigh, whereby the upper body leans slightly forward.

DIE FREIE HUT (The Free Guard)

From the Cod. icon. 394a

"Der statt in der fryen hutt"

The Free Guard is only shown in the Cod. icon. 394a. It has a passive character and is well suited to meet an attack by the opponent. Although a rather broad stance is shown in the Cod. icon. 394, we interpret it as shoulder-wide, for an excessively broad stance is simply makes one too lethargic to react. The ability to react is decisive when awaiting an attack if one is to be able to counter it successfully.

The stance is thus shoulder-wide with knees slightly bent. We stand facing the opponent, with the feet parallel on a line or splayed slightly. The dagger is held crosswise in front of the body at crotch level, with the elbows slightly bent. Thus the arms are not straightened. If the arms were straightened, we would first have to gain momentum to react powerfully to a low attack. That costs time and does not contribute to a successful defense.

This guard is very well suited to executing the Upper and Lower Shield, but Reaching Over can also be executed effectively from it.

DER ZWIFFELSTICH

From the Cod. icon. 394a

"So halt sich der im zwiffelstich und hat der Tegen uff dem Rucken und mag stechen mit welicher hand er wyl"

The Zwiffelstich is also found only in the Cod. icon. 394a. The stance is somewhat more than shoulder-wide, with the left leg forward. The knees are slightly bent. The weight rests more on the front foot. The front foot points toward the opponent, the back foot faces forward at an angle of about 45 degrees. The upper body is held parallel to the opponent and bent slightly forward.

The dagger is held in both hands behind the back—with the point facing downward. The opponent should be left in the dark as to which hand will be used to attack. This can be seen as an argument for practice in wielding the dagger with both hands, for otherwise this position would be completely valueless.

As this guard has little defensive potential, once it has been assumed one should not wait too long to attack. The Zwiffelstich is a guard that is much better suited for the attack than defense, but this should not mean that a defense from it is not possible.

DIE OBERE GEWAPPNETE HUT (The Upper Forearmed Guard)

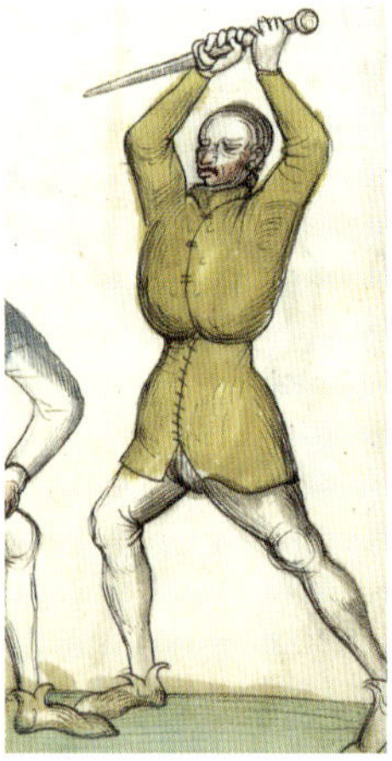

From the KK 5342

"Das ist der viert stich gewappet"

The Upper Forearmed Guard is found in the KK 5342, the Ms. Chart A558 and the 78A15. The left leg is in the forward position and bears the majority of the body weight. The stance is roughly shoulder-width and upright. The back leg pushes forward, and the arms are raised above the head. The front foot faces toward the opponent and the back foot faces the front at an angle of about 45 degrees. The dagger is gripped in both hands and is held short. The right hand encircles the pommel, and the left hand is near the blade. Incidentally, in the KK 5342, the right hand is near the blade, while in the Ms. Chart A558, it is the left. The knees are bent slightly. The threat from this guard is a powerful stab from above.

DIE UNTERE GEWAPPNETE HUT (The Lower Forearmed Guard)

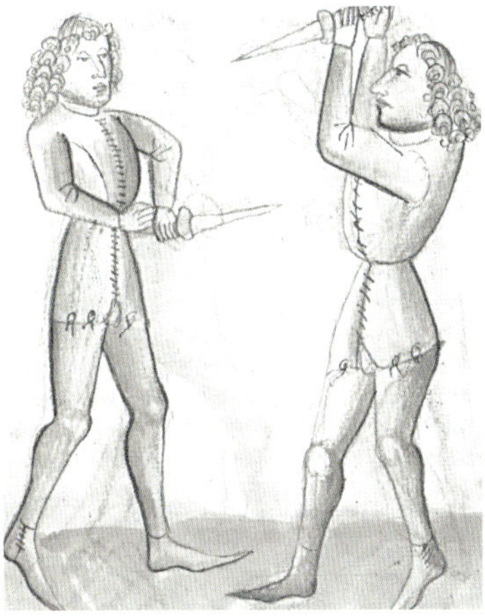

From the Ms. Chart. A 558

The Lower Forearmed Guard is only found in the Ms. Chart A558. The right leg is in the forward position and bears the majority of the body weight. The front foot faces toward the opponent and the back foot faces the front at an angle of about 45 degrees. The stance is roughly shoulder-width and upright, and the back leg pushes forward.

The arms are held in front of the abdomen with the dagger, whose point faces the opponent. The dagger is held in both hands. The right hand fully encompasses the pommel, and the left hand rests on the dagger's head disc in order to powerfully assist the stab from behind. The threat from this guard is a powerful stab at the middle of the body.

DIE MITTLERE HUT (The Middle Guard)

From the Ms. Chart. A 558

The Middle Guard is only depicted in the Ms. Chart A558. One could view it as a free fight guard. The stance is shoulder wide, with the weight equally distributed on both feet. The left foot is forward and pointing toward the opponent, while the back foot faces the front at an angle of about 45 degrees. The dagger is held in front of the body at about waist height and extended slightly forward. The knees are slightly bent. In his fencing manual "*Gründtliche Beschreibung des Fechtens,*" Meyer describes the Middle Guard and the Side Guard as identical with respect to the possibilities from them.

DER ANFANG IM RINGEN, GESCHLOSSEN (The Beginning in Wrestling, Closed)

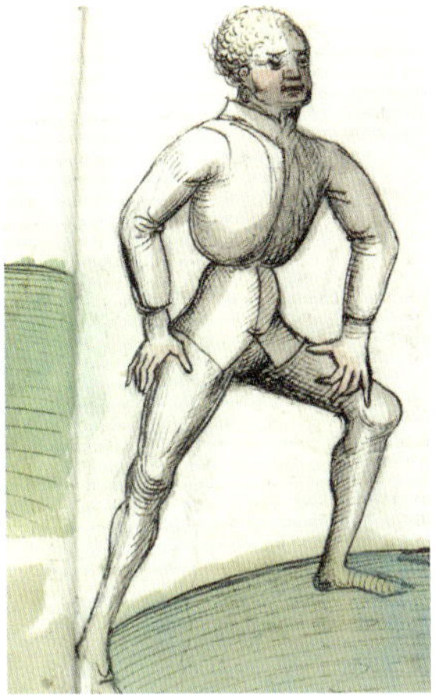

From the KK 5342

"Der Anfang im Ringen"

The stance is about shoulder-wide. One foot is slightly farther forward, and the knees are bent. In this guard, as in the next, it makes almost no difference which foot leads. The front foot points at the opponent, the back faces forward at an angle of about 45 degrees. The upper body is almost parallel to the opponent, with the left side leading slightly. The upper body is bent forward slightly, and the hands are on the left and right thighs.

DER ANFANG IM RINGEN, OFFEN (The Beginning in Wrestling, Open)

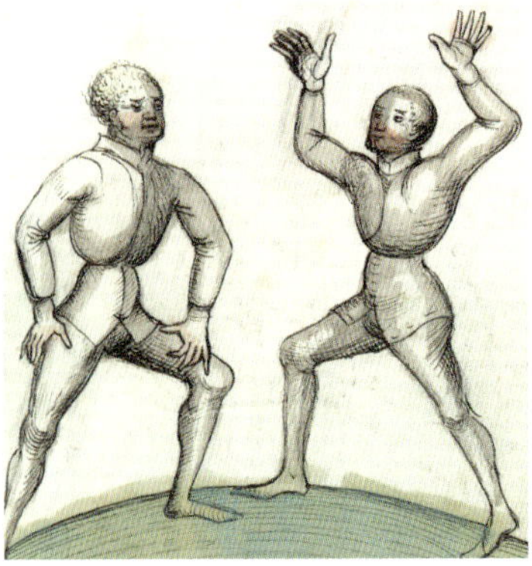

From the KK 5342

"Der Anfang im Ringen"

The stance is somewhat more than shoulder-wide. One foot is slightly farther forward. The knees are bent, and the upper body is parallel to the opponent. The front foot faces the opponent, and the back foot faces the front at an angle of about 45 degrees. The body weight is slightly more on the front leg. The back leg is under tension, so as to be able to race forward. The arms are held high, but not fully extended, instead slightly bent. They are also extended to the sides slightly.

4.2 The Displacements

In the following, all of the techniques that stop an opponent's attack are called displacements. The various displacements can have quite different objectives, however. In some, a displacement in the usual sense is made and the opponent's attack is braked quite forcefully. Others, on the other hand, merely deflect it gently to the side, and still others strive to knock the opponent's arm away. As well there are displacements whose intent is to capture the opponent's attack.

Grasping the arms and also capturing the hand (not the Capture as such) are surely not displacements in the true sense. They are rather the start of several techniques. Nevertheless, they serve to stop an attack. As a beginner, one should exclude them from the overall technique and practice them separately. That is why we include them here. While we depict the displacements with an armed defender, they can also be executed by an unarmed combatant.

DAS FANGEN (The Capture)

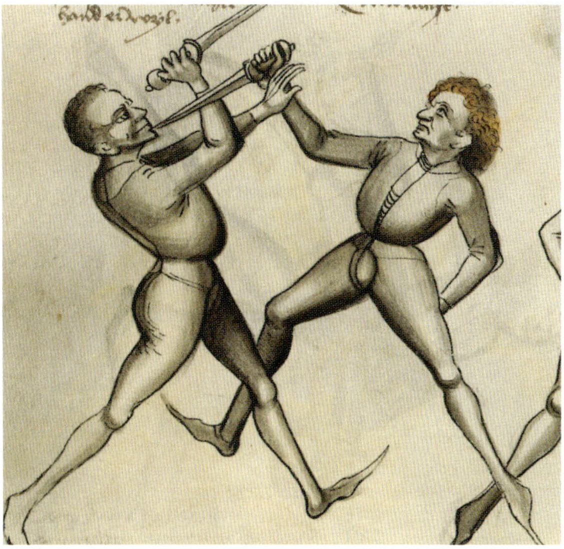

From the Cod. icon. 394a

As the name suggests, the purpose of the Capture is to capture the opponent's dagger hand. The dagger hand and the free hand form a V, in which the opponent's attack is intercepted. The free hand arm rests beneath the arm of the dagger hand. Although, in the manuscripts, the Capture is only used against attacks from the From the Roof Guard, it can also used to capture attacks from other directions.

1 Ralf is in the From the Roof Guard. Clemens awaits the attack in the Ebich. Both are holding their daggers short. If Ralf takes a step forward and comes down from the From the Roof Guard, Clemens takes a step forward to counter the attack.

2 Clemens raises his weapon arm, thrusts over Ralf's stab, and with it pushes Ralf's dagger arm to the side (right). He then brings his left arm under his own dagger arm, in order to form the V and capture the opponent's dagger arm.

3 When Ralf's weapon arm is in this V, Clemens brings his dagger over the opponent's wrist and seizes his own blade with his free left hand in order to exert pressure on the opponent's arm. Strictly speaking, this is the Skerry. The segment until the V is closed is the Capture. We can say that the Skerry begins after the closing of the V.

4 There are two ways of capturing the opponent's arm, both of which are found in Master Talhoffer's manuscripts. One is to capture the opponent's dagger outside one's crossed arms, on one's own left forearm—as shown in the photos—or between the crossed arms. To do this, as soon as one moves one's left hand under the weapon arm to form the V, one must simultaneously move to the right. This automatically causes the opponent's dagger to go between the arms.

Catching the dagger between one's own arms, without first moving the weapon arm to the side, basically also works. It can happen, however, that the opponent's dagger still reaches its target, even if not completely. It is therefore advisable to first direct the opponent's dagger to the side.

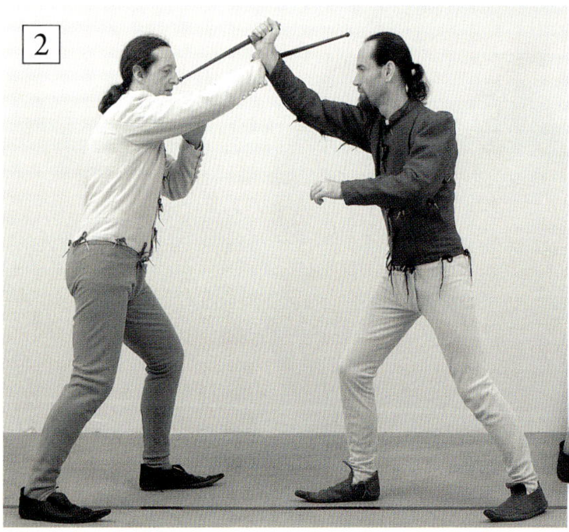

Clemens stabs over Ralf's weapon arm …

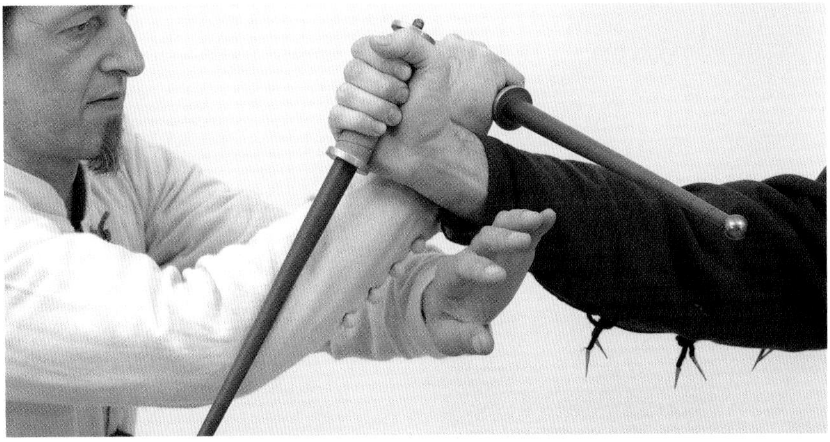

… passes his free hand under his own and Ralf's …

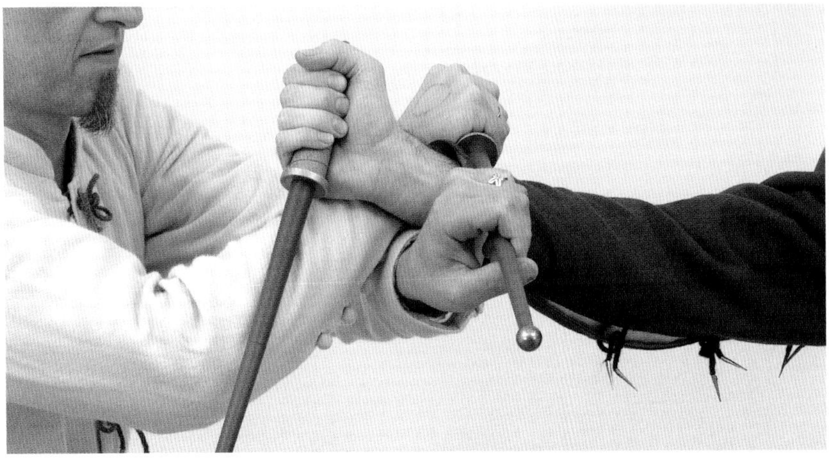

… and grasps the blade of his own dagger.

DER OBERE SCHILT (The Upper Shield)

The Upper Shield is a hard block against attacks from above. Master Talhoffer expressly states that the block should be pushed when executing the Shield. If the opponent has a long dagger, care must be taken to keep the arms extended and slightly to the side when blocking, as a very long dagger or a very powerful attack might be able to reach the face despite the block.

1 Ralf is in the Free Guard and is holding the dagger long. Clemens comes with an attack from the From the Roof Guard and is holding his dagger short.

2 If Clemens attacks from above, Ralf takes a small step toward the attack and drives his Shield, offset slightly to the right or left, under the forearm of Clemens' weapon arm. He thus blocks the opponent's arm, not his dagger. This is very effective if one strikes the bones of the attacker's wrist. The forearm as such is somewhat less sensitive.

It is important not to spring at the attacker with the Shield raised; for if he recognizes what the defender has in mind, he will change his attack. When employing not just the Shield, but in general any defense, it is therefore important to delay acting for as long as possible. But of course not until it is too late …

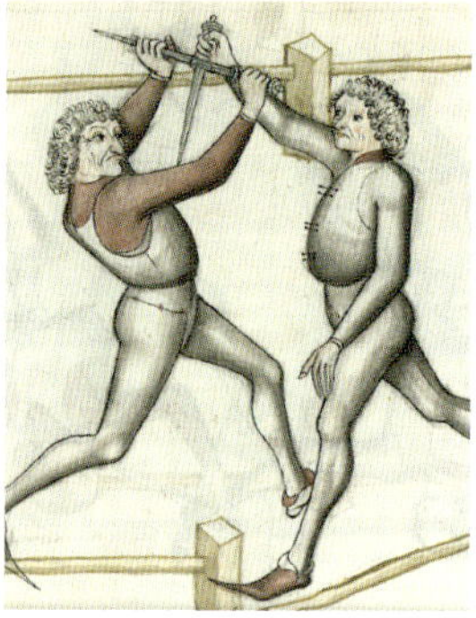

From the Thott 290 2°

"Der ober schilt"

1

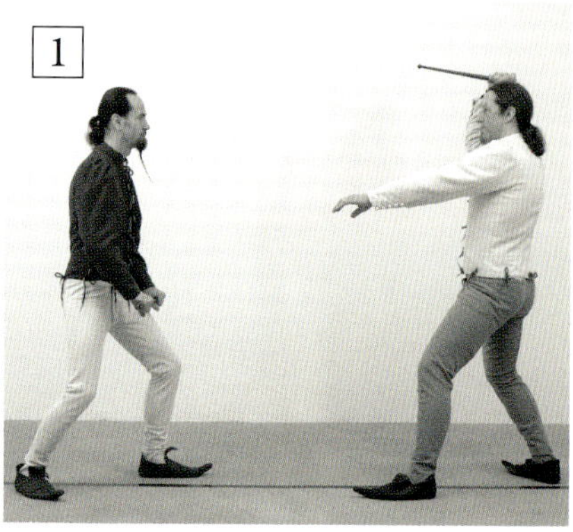

2

DER UNTERE SCHILT (The Lower Shield)

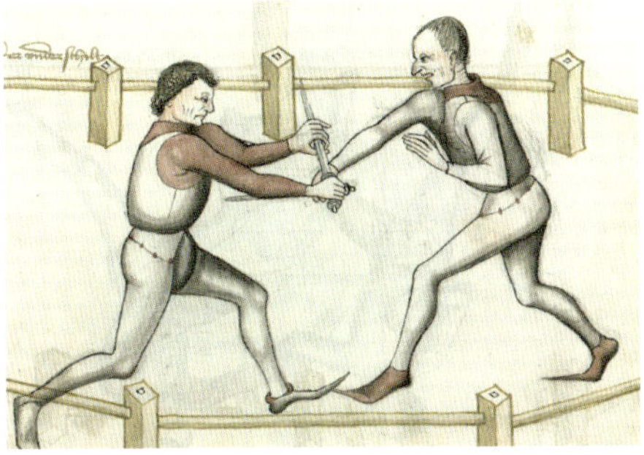

From the Thott 290 2°

"Der under schilt"

1 Clemens is in the From the Roof Guard and is holding the dagger long. Ralf comes from the Zwiffelstich with a stab at the abdomen, also holding the dagger long. When the stab comes, Clemens steps his right foot back and slightly to the side. As he does so, he brings his dagger horizontally to Ralf's attacking dagger, in order to grasp the front part of the blade with his left hand.

2 With his dagger, he then powerfully blocks Ralf's attacking forearm. Here too, it is advisable to extend the arm and block as far away from one's own body as possible and not stand directly behind the block. It also makes sense to move the abdomen back a little. Otherwise a particularly fast or powerful stab might still catch the defender despite all his efforts.

DAS ÜBERGREIFEN (Reaching Over)

From the Cod. icon. 394a

"Der hat den äbich angebunden und wyl In übergryffen"

1 Clemens is in the From the Roof Guard and is holding the dagger long.

2 When the stab comes From the Roof, Ralf steps his left foot to the left while also moving his upper body slightly to the left. The right foot remains where it is.

3 As he steps out, Ralf makes a circular movement with his weapon arm, like a clockwise-turning windmill.

4 In this way, Ralf reaches over the attacking weapon arm, catching it and pressing it against his side, with the result that the opponent's weapon arm is clamped between Ralf's side and his arm. The one reaching over should be sure to catch the opponent's arm as close to his own armpit as possible. If the arm is caught further below the armpit, it is no longer possible to hold it really securely.

That is Reaching Over from the outside. Reaching Over works equally well from the inside. Lignitzer[1], for example, often Reaches Over from the left in order to then make a stab.

[1]Peter von Danzig: Transcription and Translation of the Manuscript 44 A 8, VS-Books, ISBN 978-3-932077-34-0.

3

4

FÜR DEN UNTEREN STICH (For the Lower Stab)

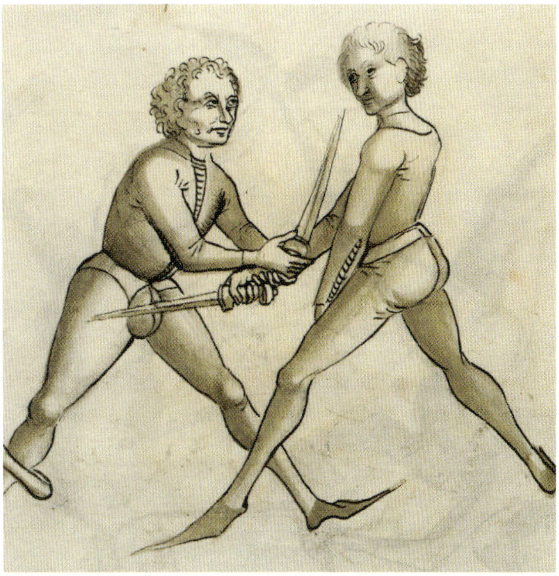

From the Cod. icon. 394a

This block is shown in Master Talhoffer's manuscripts both armed (from the defender's point of view) and unarmed.

1 Ralf is in the Zwiffelstich and is holding the dagger long. Clemens is in the From the Roof Guard with the dagger held long.

2 When Ralf stabs at the abdomen, Clemens steps his left foot back (sidestepping to the left is also possible) …

3 … and grasps Ralf's attacking wrist with both hands from the left and right. You will discover what can happen from there later in the book.

A simultaneous sidestep is strongly advisable. For if the attacker is very quick or something goes wrong with the Capture, it is not a mistake if one has sidestepped out of the line of attack.

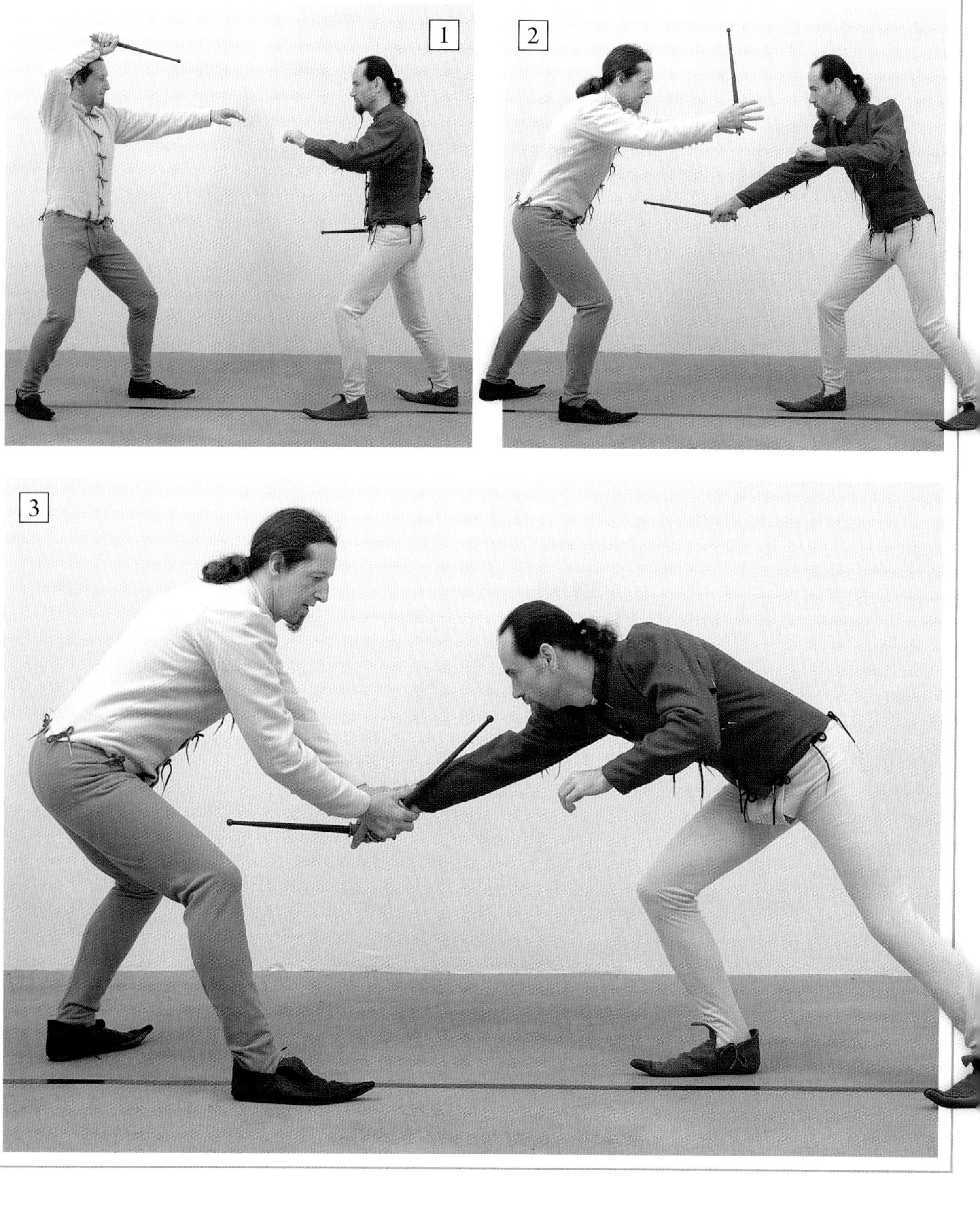
1
2
3

FÜR DEN OBERN STICH (For the Upper Stab)

From the Thott 290 2°

"Für den obern stich Mit dem linggen arme"

1 Ralf is in the From the Roof Guard with dagger held short, as is Clemens. If Clemens makes a stab from above, Ralf evades by moving forward and slightly to the left.

2 As he does so, he raises his left arm to block Clemens's forearm between his weapon arm and dagger, subsequently grasping the elbow of Clemens's weapon arm with his left hand.

3 After grasping Clemens's elbow, Ralf pulls it toward him. This leaves him free to stab wherever he wishes to.

DIE HAND GREIFEN, AUSSEN (Grasp the Hand, Outside)

1

1 Ralf makes a stab from the From the Roof Guard, holding the dagger short. Clemens is in the Free Guard and is thus holding the dagger long.

2 When the stab comes, Clemens takes a step back with his right foot, raises his left arm and takes Ralf's attacking arm just behind the wrist. Clemens is equally well able to intercept the attack by taking a step back with his left foot. The only difference is that, because of the different angle between the dagger and wrist, Clemens reaches for the outside of Ralf's wrist.

3 The capturer's finger is a tricky matter here, for if one reaches for the attacking arm with the open hand and does not capture it correctly, the result can be a dislocated or broken finger. When intercepting the arm, therefore, contact with it should be established with the inner edge of the hand while pushing it away as little as possible. Only then do the fingers grasp the arm. The main purpose of pushing the arm away as little as possible is not to change its direction. Rather it is to occupy the opponent's arm until, after contact is made, the fingers are spread in order to seize the arm or wrist.

In one technique in the Ms. Chart A558, the hand is also grasped with the weapon hand, in which the capturer holds his own dagger.

2

Close-Up

3

Close-up of the hand during Capture: to avoid finger injury, first make contact with the attacking arm using the flat of the hand with fingers together. Only then are the fingers spread to properly grasp the wrist.

DIE HAND GREIFEN, INNEN (Grasp the Hand, Inside)

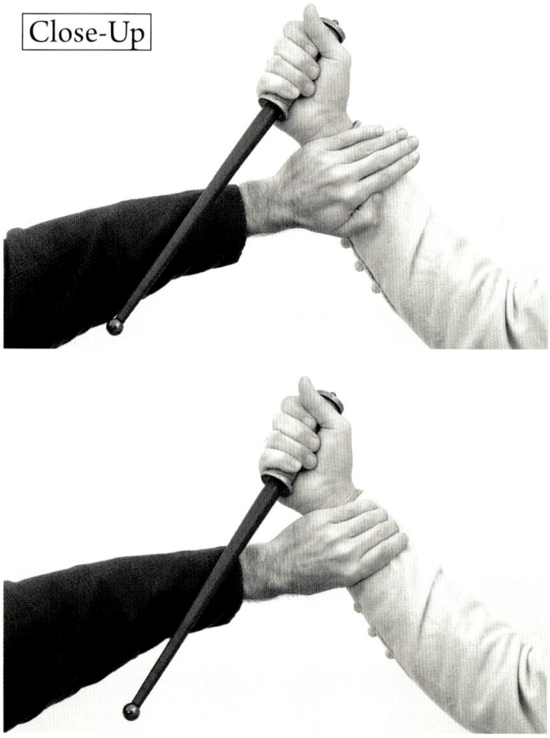

The fingers are held straight when first seizing the weapon hand. Only after contact is made do they grip the opponent's wrist.

1 Holding the dagger short, Clemens attempts to stab from the From the Roof Guard. Ralf is standing in the same position.

2 When the stab comes, Ralf takes a short step out of line with his left foot, raises his left arm and captures Clemens's attacking arm just behind the wrist.

3 Here too the flat of the hand makes first contact with the attacking arm with fingers together and in the process pushes it to the left slightly. Only then are the fingers spread to grip properly.

WEGSCHLAGEN OBEN (Swat Upward)

1 Ralf is in the From the Roof Guard and is holding the dagger short. Clemens is in the Free Guard and is also holding the dagger short.

2 When Ralf makes stabs from above, Clemens steps his left leg out of the line of attack. As he does so he also moves his upper body slightly to the left to gain momentum and subsequently be able to employ his entire body.

3 He lets go of his blade with his left hand, in order to throw up his right arm. With the arm he makes a circular clockwise motion and with the fist grasping the grip of his dagger strikes at Ralf's attacking arm. The energy for swatting the arm away should come from the hips and not the arm alone.

WEGSCHLAGEN UNTEN (Swat Downward)

1 Clemens comes from the Zwiffelstich and is holding his dagger long. Ralf is in the From the Roof Guard and is also holding his dagger long.

2 If the stab is aimed at the abdomen, Ralf sidesteps to the left by stepping to the left with his left leg.

3 At the same time, in a circular movement he strikes at Clemens's attacking arm with the fist of his weapon arm. In this way this attack is also swatted to the side. Here too the swatting motion should originate from the hips.

4.3 The Stabs

In the KK 5342 the body positions that are otherwise generally called guards are also called stabs or thrusts (*Stiche*). Therein we can see basic stabs, or positions from which the basic stabs are executed. In the Cod. icon. 394a the guard in which the dagger is held behind the back is called the *Zwiffelstich*, consequently it must be seen as a stab. Of course we can also deliver a stab from the guards that are not expressly called "stabs."

When preparing for a stab there are different approaches with respect to body position. For one, when attacking we can make ourselves very long. Before the stab, the right leg and the weapon in the right hand are back. If we now initiate a stab, both the right hand and right foot come forward.

This has the advantage of bestowing great range. A disadvantage, for example, is that the second, unarmed hand is not fully available to counter actions by the opponent. As well, if one works straight forward, one exposes oneself to both hands to the defender. This type of attack also takes a long time, and the defender has a relatively long time to prepare for it.

Another possibility is to position the right leg and the weapon hand forward and to make the attack while taking a step forward with the left foot (for a right-hander). In this way the left hand is also fully available. It brings with it, however, the disadvantage of shortened range and a less than optimal delivery of power.

A third possibility is to position the right leg and the weapon hand forward and to leave them there. When approaching the opponent, one only moves forward with gliding steps. Joachim Meyer recommends this in his fencing manual.[1] While this results in shortened range, the attack comes very quickly and delivery of power is also very good. In our opinion this is the best method for movement in the free fight and the real thing.

There are also several possibilities in the direction from which one initiates a stab. When preparing to stab we can select the direct route and move straight toward the opponent, exposing us to both of his hands as just stated. When stabbing we can attack his left side. His weapon hand will have to cover a greater distance to make a counter-stab, which creates time for us. On the other hand, we walk straight into his free hand.

When stabbing we can also approach the side where he holds his weapon—which, of course, is not entirely without danger as we are walking into his weapon. On the other hand, one can break a stab with the free left hand as soon as it begins and is also farther away from his free hand.

As one can see, every variant has its advantage but also its disadvantage. One must decide from case to case which disadvantage one can accept, or which advantage one needs. But in any case one should always step to the side when making an attack. To make the techniques more visible in the photos, we have dispensed with this in the attacks. They should, however, absolutely be included in practice!

No matter to which side one steps, it is the result of footwork. As it is inadvisable to turn one's back to the opponent, in attacks in which one steps forward with the right leg one should step to the opponent's left. If one steps forward to the left, then step to the opponent's right.

For the depiction of the techniques in this book we have decided to begin the attacks from a broad measure. We think this makes more sense for the first basic exercises than a close measure. Of course one can employ the various stabs from any of the guards. The possibilities are almost limitless. But each guard has only one stab, for which it is really best suited.

It is best if one of the combatants remains static during training, while the other practices stabbing this "dummy." We also recommend that you practice the stabs so that they stop just short of the opponent

[1] Bavarian State Library: Meyer, Joachim: Gründtliche Beschreibung des Fechtens

or barely touch him. It is worthwhile to be able to control his weapon. In the free fight at the latest, your partner will be grateful if he does not have to completely carry out the stabs. But it also makes sense to make the stabs calmly but with more force. If possible the "victim" should also wear protective clothing.

One can also fashion soft daggers, made of cloth for example, especially for stabbing practice. We have made such practice daggers simply by rolling up bits of cloth and then wrapping them with tape (instructions may be found in the appendix). That is sufficiently stiff. In this way one can stab with full force, but must not fear injuring the other. We would only advise against stabbing into the unprotected face. If no partner is available, a tree works very well. The consequences of a stab delivered more forcefully than planned are also not as serious.

When approaching the opponent in preparation for a stab, the front foot is not the first to move (provided we are taking a full step forward), for that signals to the opponent that an attack is coming. First the back foot comes forward and is pointed at the opponent. Not until the moment that one stabs, does the back foot line up and turn somewhat to the rear. Much of the force available to us when stabbing comes from this movement. When stabbing, be certain that you stab from the body! The power must not come from the arms, but from the entire body.

The term power is slightly confusing. The most important thing is the flow of movements: the entire body must move, not just individual limbs. Pure power is rather restrictive when stabbing. If we stab with all our force, we strain the musculature more than is necessary for the movement. This only makes the attack slower.

For the attack speed is much more important than power. Ultimately we do not want to box in our opponent, rather stab him. Tests have shown that it does not require a great deal of strength to stick a pointed dagger into a piece of flesh, as long as it does not strike bone. A stab delivered quickly already has considerable force potential without having to consciously apply force. Therefore one should deliver an attack in a relaxed manner but quickly. Do not stiffen the wrist until just before the blade strikes and stab deliberately so as not to allow the attack to slide or leave its intended path. Of course an attack should not come in a wavy line, but instead go straight into the target as smoothly as possible.

1 The First Stab comes from the From the Roof Guard, with the dagger held short. The right foot is back, as is the raised dagger arm.

2 We now move toward the opponent with a step forward with the right foot and stab at him. As we do so, we step slightly toward the opponent's left side.

3 The target of our attack is the opponent's face, the right side of his neck or the right upper breast.

DER ERSTE STICH (The First Stab)

From the KK 5342

" Das ist der ober stich und der erst"

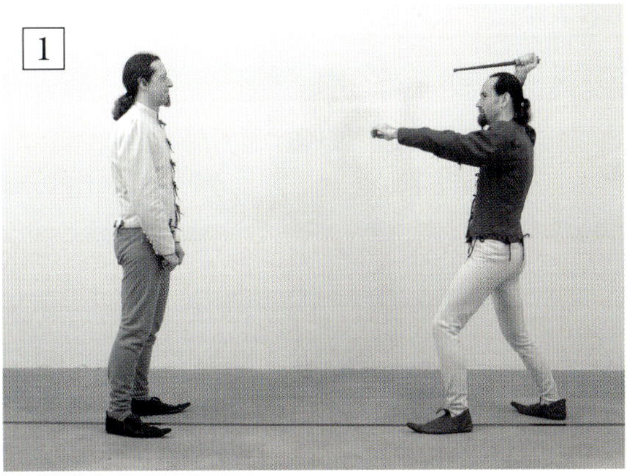

This stab is the kind of attack seen most often in the manuscripts.

That is apparently a peculiarity of the Middle Ages. If one watches videos of present-day knife attacks, they almost always show a stab at the abdomen with the knife held long. In the Middle Ages, attacks were often made with the dagger held short, because it was worn on the right side of the belt, where it was more easily drawn with the short grip.

DER EBICH-STICH (The Ebich Stab)

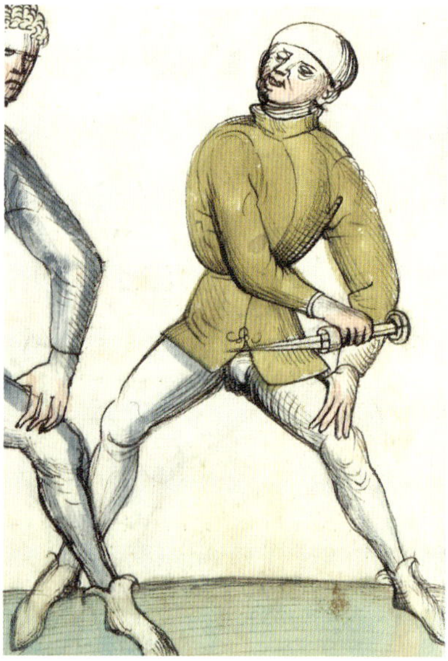

From the KK 5342

"Der ist der ebich stich und der under"

1 The only stab that automatically brings our free left hand forward with it, in order to parry the opponent's counterattack.

2 The back foot comes forward and steps left toward the opponent. At the same time the free hand moves in the direction of the opponent's dagger so as to be able to block it. Alternatively we slide forward and leave the right foot forward. The stab is made upward and is aimed at the abdominal area, the lower ribs or under the opponent's chin.

DER DRITTE STICH (The Third Stab)

From the KK 5342

"Der stat in der undern hut In dem dritten stich"

1 The right foot is back and moves forward with the stab.

2 We move out slightly to the right to begin the stab. The free hand is held forward and remains there to protect us against counterattacks. In general one should always move the second, free hand with the weapon hand. Master Meyer also advises this in his fencing manual[1]. He recommends that in every action the free hand be moved with the dagger, in order to be able to protect the dagger with it at all times. The stab is aimed straight at the opponent's abdomen.

[1]Bavarian State Library: Meyer, Joachim: Gründtliche Beschreibung des Fechtens.

DER DRITTE STICH (The Third Stab)

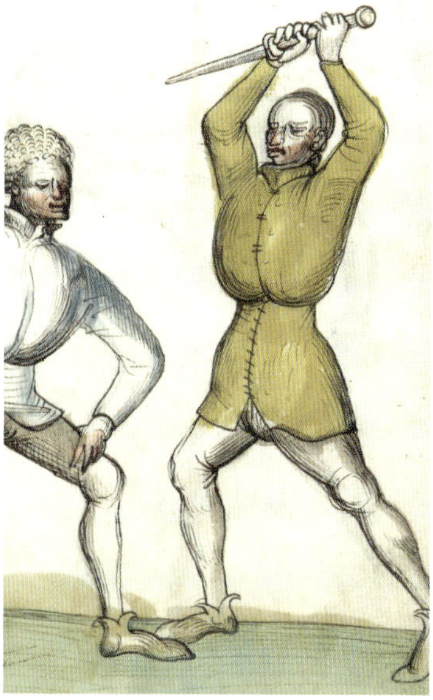

From the KK 5342

"Das ist der viert stich gewappet"

1 The right foot moves forward. One steps out to the right slightly to begin the stab at the opponent.

2 If one initiates this stab at the opponent, the second hand is absent for capturing opposing actions. The advantage of this stab is that it is very powerful. One can thus simply sweep an opponent's stab to the side with one's own stab or perhaps even penetrate light armor.

DER UNTERE GEWAPPNETE STICH (The Lower Forearmed Stab)

From the Ms. Chart. A 558

1 To begin the stab, step the left foot forward while moving slightly out of line to the left.

2 The inevitable follows: a stab to the abdomen. Apart from the fact that both hands are bound, the Lower Forearmed Stab has the disadvantage that, because of the position of the arms, it has a very short range. Of course Master Talhoffer would have had something to say about this, but what?

DER ZWIFFELSTICH

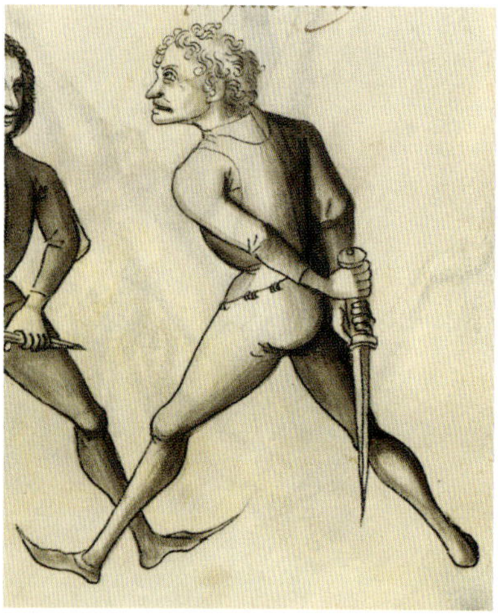

From the Cod. icon. 394a

"So halt sich der Im zwiffelstich und hat den Tegen uff dem Rucken und mag stechen mit welicher hand er wyl"

1

2

1 The dagger is held behind the back. The left foot slides forward one step. In doing so, one also steps out of line to the left. One can just as well step the right foot forward. The strength of this stab lies in the fact that the opponent does not know with which hand the stab will ultimately come. One should therefore delay bringing the dagger out from behind one's back for as long as possible, but in any case before one comes within range of the opponent. Otherwise one forfeits the second hand, which might be needed to defend against an opposing counterattack in an emergency.

2 The Zwiffelstich shows us that we should also practice wielding the dagger in the left hand. It can happen that the right arm is injured or the right hand is caught in a lever and one must take the dagger in one's left hand. In short, one should also practice stabbing with the left hand. And not just stabbing: one can and should also practice the other techniques with the left hand. Every additional thing that one can do helps in the real thing. It certainly cannot hurt.

DER HERZSTICH (Stab to the Heart)

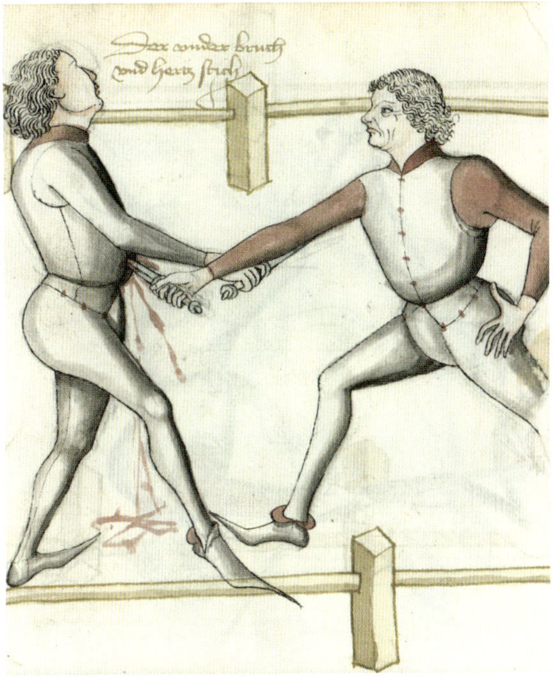

From the Thott 290 2°

"Der under bruch und hertz stich"

1 The right foot steps forward and to the side. The stab is made upward at the opponent's abdomen. The Stab to the Heart is actually not a special stab. It can be delivered from the Zwiffelstich or the Lower Guard. The special thing about it is that it is delivered from below like a boxer's hook.

2 The dagger stabs from low to high, in order to pierce the opponent's abdomen and, travelling upward, seek the heart.

From the KK 5342

Chapter 5: The Counter-Stabs

We understand counter-stab to mean countering an opponent's attack by means of a stab. Counter-stabs are significantly less complicated than the more complex levers and throws, which we will delve into later. They are often the first thing that works in a free fight.

In Master Talhoffer's manuscripts we find dagger techniques that are very complicated and represent a very high level of the art of dagger fencing. One should not forget, however, that above all else a dagger is there simply for stabbing. One should not ignore this point, for a simple stab to the body is often the simplest way.

STECHEN ODER SCHLAGEN (Stab or Strike)

1 Clemens attacks Ralf with a stab from the From the Roof Guard but holds his dagger long.

2 When the stab comes from above, Ralf raises his left arm high and captures the opponent's forearm with his left hand.

3 Ralf initially blocks the arm with his fingers together. Only after making contact do the fingers grip.

4 Ralf twists Clemens's arm out and to the side.

5 6 If Clemens now brings his free arm forward to begin a counter-action, Ralf strikes at his hand from above with his dagger.

7 Then he allows the movement to change from a blow to a stab. He does not pull the dagger back while doing so. As soon as the blow on Clemens's hand is completed, Ralf immediately thrusts his dagger at Clemens's body.

From the Cod. icon. 394a

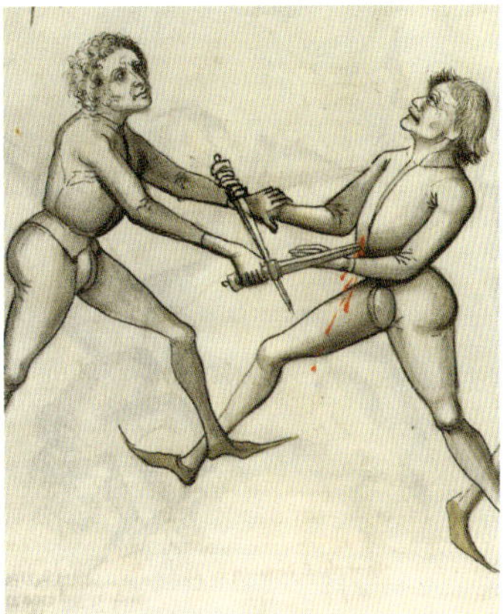

"Für den obern stich so würff din lincken arm uff und fach sin Stich uff den lincken arm und macht mit dinem Tegen stechen oder slahen. – Als Ich hon gestochen, So ist es mir gebrochen"

2

3

4

5

6

7

DEM STICH HINWEG HELFEN
(Help the Stab Across)

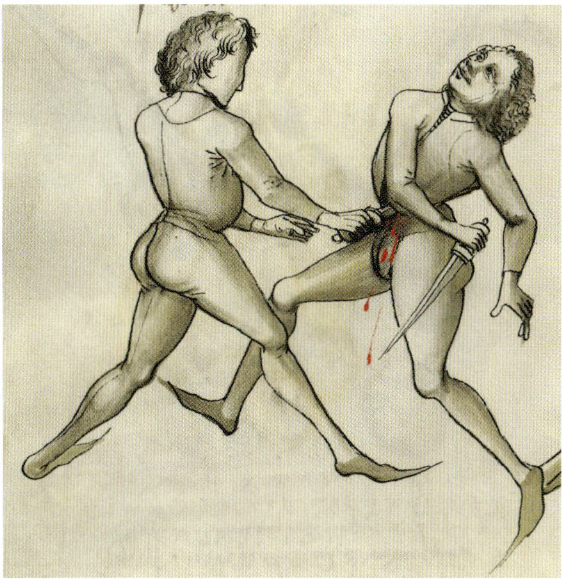

From the Cod. icon. 394a

"Für den obern stich hatt er sinen rechten Arm uff geworfen und sinem Stich hinweg geholffen und ersticht In. – Der hatt gestochen und Ist Im der stich gebrochen"

1

1 Ralf comes with a stab from the Roof. Clemens awaits the attack in the Free Guard.

2 When the stab comes from above, Clemens steps his left foot out of line to the left. As he does so, he lets go of his blade with his left hand, throws up his right hand with the dagger and blocks the stab.

3 This time, however, the block is made so powerfully that the attack is swept aside. To develop sufficient force, it is not enough to simply raise the arm. Instead the blocking arm must be brought up in a circular motion into which one puts the correct momentum. Clemens describes such a clockwise movement with his right arm. At its end, Clemens' forearm strikes Ralf's forearm.

4 Clemens thus sweeps the attacking arm to the side. The movement does not end here, however. Clemens continues the circle until the tip of his blade is in front of Ralf's abdomen. Then Clemens simply drives his dagger forward, directly into Ralf's abdomen, while stepping forward with his right foot.

5 The entire block, including the stab, has something of a corkscrew-like motion, with which Clemens "screws" his dagger into Ralf's abdomen.

DER GEWALTSTICH (The Power Stab)

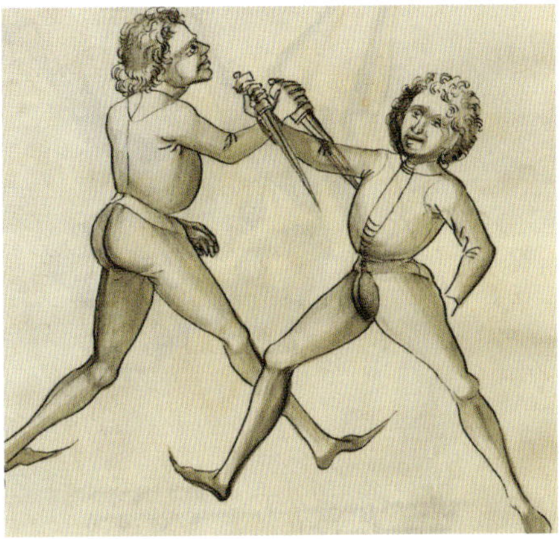

From the Cod. icon. 394a

"Das soll sin ain vahen usz der schäre den arm oder dem hals" Author's note: we were unable to do anything with the text accompanying the illustration of this technique. We could not see anything in the picture that even remotely resembled a Schäre, neither on the arm or neck. Instead in the illustration we saw a stab, which is illustrated in the following pictures.

1 Clemens comes with a stab from the From the Roof Guard. Ralf awaits the attack in the Ebich.

2 When Clemens stabs at Ralf from above, the latter steps far out to the left with his left foot, and immediately moves his right foot forward toward Clemens.

3 As he does so, he stabs at Clemens's chest. When making this stab, Ralf pushes the attacking arm of the attacker to the side through the power of his stab. Clemens is thus prevented from beginning a stab of his own.

4 Ralf employs his entire body when stabbing. He puts his weight into the stab in order to force Clemens's arm to the side.

3

4

VOM DACH GESTOCHEN
(Stabbed From the Roof)

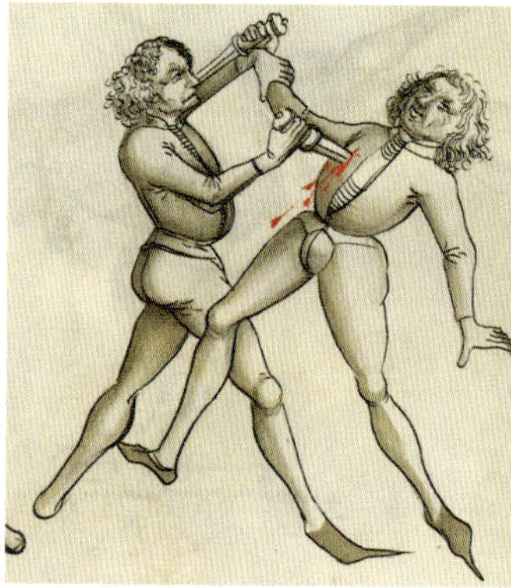

From the Cod. icon. 394a

"So hat der versetzt mit dem lincken Arm und Sticht och von Tach. – Als der gestochen hat von Tach"

1

1 Both have assumed the From the Roof Guard.

2 If Ralf attacks with a stab from above, Clemens moves his left foot out to the left and forward. He blocks the stab with his forearm and seeks Ralf's elbow with his hand in order to grasp it. As he moves out to the side, Clemens takes the seized arm with him, opening Ralf's right side.

3 While pulling the seized elbow towards him slightly, Clemens steps his right foot close behind Ralf's right leg. He now stabs at Ralf's chest.

2

3

DER OBERE BRUCH (The Upper Break)

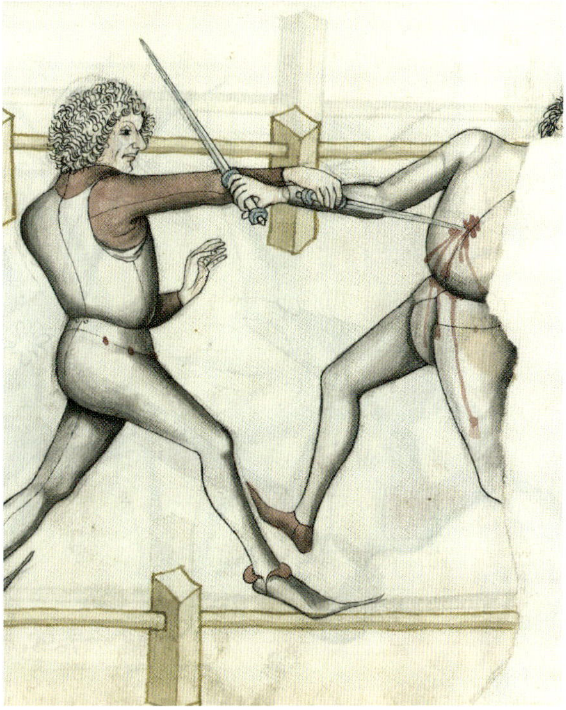

From the Thott 290 2°

"Der bruch und dot stich"

1

1 Clemens comes with a stab from the Roof Guard. Ralf awaits the attack in the Lower Guard.

2 When Clemens makes a stab from the From the Roof Guard, Ralf sidesteps to the left with his left foot. As he does so, with the flat of his left hand he knocks Clemens's attacking weapon arm out of the way.

3 Then he immediately takes a step to Clemens' right side with his right leg and stabs over his weapon arm at his chest.

4 In the process Ralf's stabbing arm makes contact with Clemens' weapon arm, and the stabbing energy forces it to the side. This gives him a time advantage before Clemens can return the stab.

The technique would also work if one deleted the pushing-away movement with the left arm, stepped far out to the right and courageously stabbed at the target—although the risk to the attacker would be greater.

DER UNTERE BRUCH UND HERZSTICH (The Lower Break and Heart Stab)

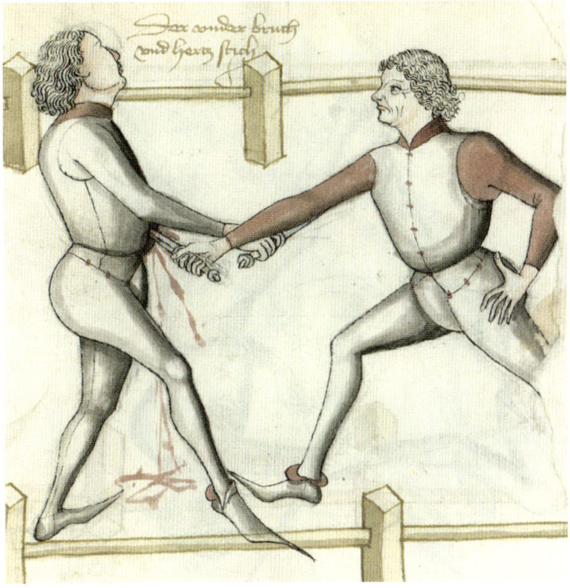

From the Thott 290 2°

"Der under bruch und hertz stich"

1 Ralf is standing in the Zwiffelstich and with his right hand stabs at Clemens' abdomen. Clemens awaits the attack in the From the Roof Guard, holding the dagger long.

2 When the stab to his abdomen comes, Clemens makes a falling-to-the-left arc-like movement with his weapon arm, from high to low. This enables him to block the attack with his fist on Ralf's right forearm.

3 Clemens continues this movement until he has swept the attack to the side and has created a path for his dagger to Ralf's abdominal area. He exploits this immediately and thrusts at Ralf's abdomen.

4 While delivering the stab, Clemens takes a step toward Ralf with his right foot. This continues to force Ralf's arm to the side.

We have also tried to simply block the stab without stepping out to the side, however this proved tricky with an upward stab from below. It sometimes works, but not always. When attempting this block, just as often we ended up on the point of the opponent's dagger.

3

4

DER MORDSTICH (The Killing Stab)

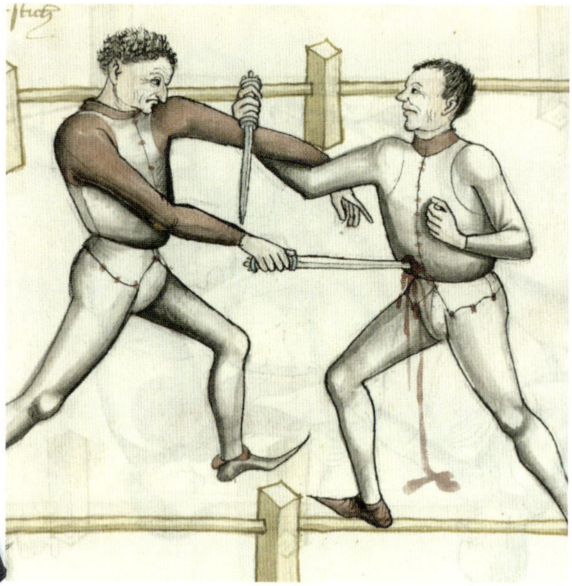

"Der mort stich"

1 Clemens is in the From the Roof Guard and intends to stab from above. Ralf awaits the attack in the Free Guard.

2 Ralf counters the stab coming from above by stepping his left foot forward and to the left. As he does so, he releases his grip on his blade with his left hand. He raises his left hand to intercept Clemens' thrust. Ralf blocks the stab with his forearm against Clemens' forearm, just behind his wrist.

3 He lets his arm fall over Clemens's arm, in order to reach around and grasp his elbow from the outside.

4 Ralf now pulls Clemens' elbow towards him, knocking him off balance, and stabs at his abdomen.

1
2
3
4

DAS WEITERFÜHREN (The Follow-Up)

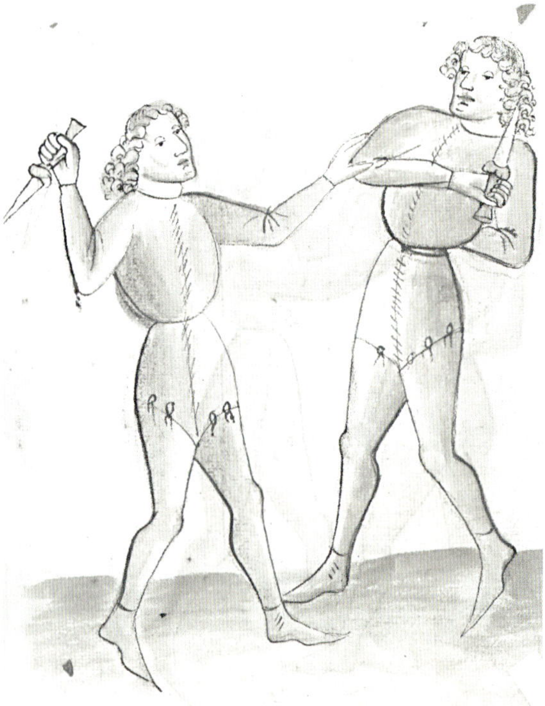

From the Ms. Chart. A 558

1 Ralf attacks with a stab from the From the Roof Guard. Clemens, who is also in the From the Roof Guard, evades by leaning his upper body backward, just before the stab reaches him.

2 As he does this, he grasps Ralf's elbow and pushes it towards him. Clemens' feet do not move when he leans backward.

3 Clemens thus evades the stab and pushes Ralf's arm to the side.

4 He then stabs at Ralf's chest.

It is not compulsory that the defender not move his feet. If the attacker gets too close, one should also take a step back.

4

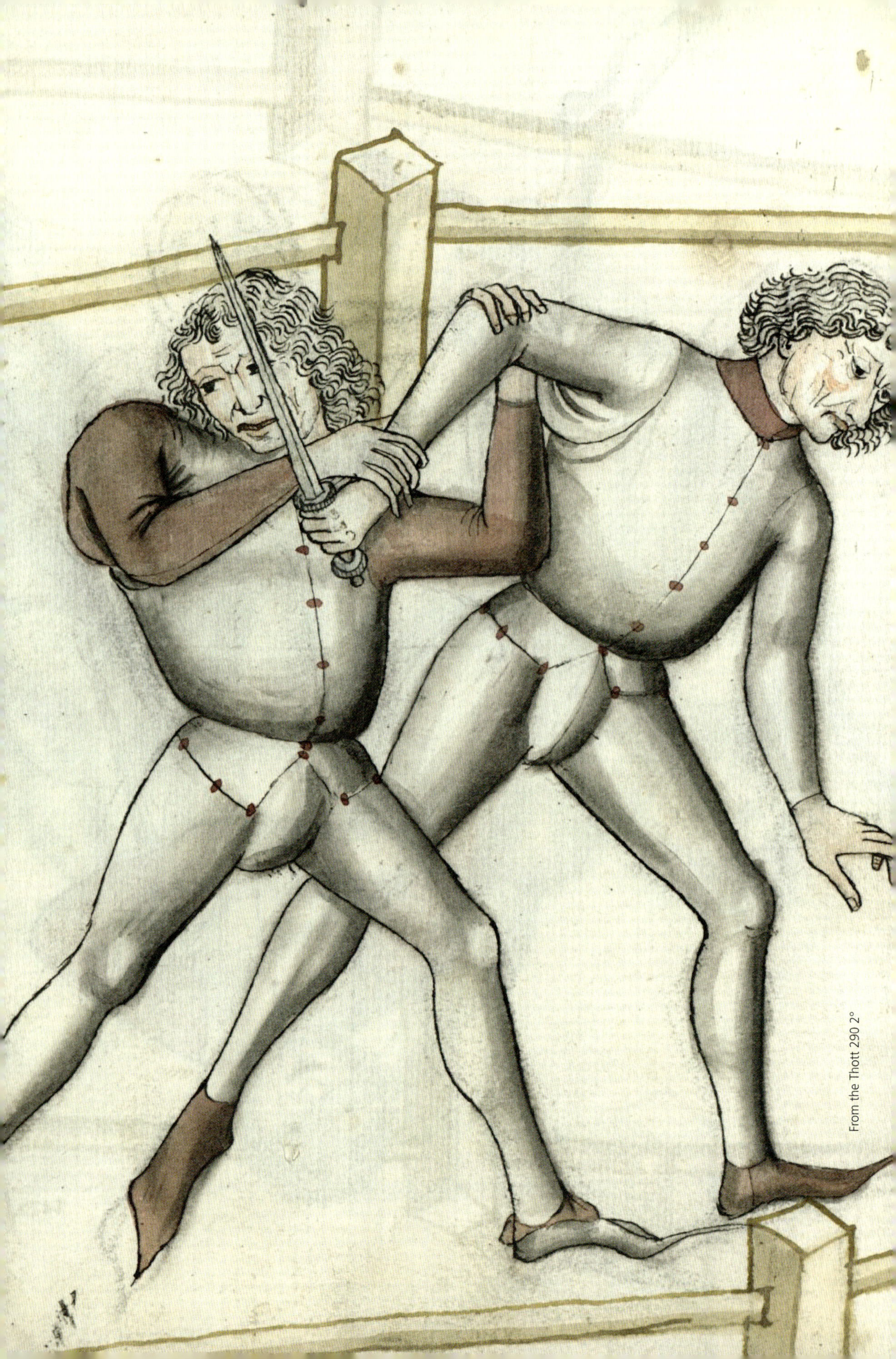

From the Thott 290 2°

Chapter 6: Unarmed against a Dagger

We will now turn to the techniques in which an unarmed fighter defends himself against an attacker wielding a dagger. In the following descriptions of the techniques, we always indicate whether the defender steps away or toward the attacker in response to his attack, but this is often variable. The reaction does not depend solely on the individual techniques, but also on how the attacker approaches the defender.

If a technique requires us to move forward, but the opponent almost runs over us as he attacks, then it makes no sense to go forward. In this case it is cleverer to evade by stepping back or to the side. One should therefore always adapt his footwork to his training partner or the actual situation, to the extent that this is possible.

You will often read, "... the other hand immediately goes." Often, if we have grabbed the opponent with one hand, we must immediately also employ the second hand to support the first, for example to grab an elbow. Master Meyer therefore recommends that the free hand should always follow the dagger hand, in order to have the free hand in position immediately if its is needed. That is good advice!

In all shoulder and elbow levers, it is important that the one executing the maneuver is standing close to the opponent. If he is too far away, the one being attacked can wrench himself out of the lever, or the technique simply will not work.

DEN ARM WÜRGEN (Choke the Arm)

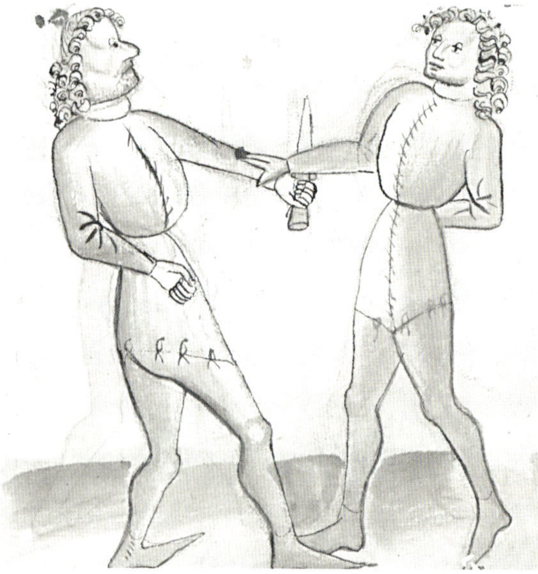

From the Ms. Chart. A 558

1 Ralf assumes the From the Roof Guard and makes a stab from above. Clemens is in the Beginning in Wrestling position and is in a closed stance.

2 When the stab comes down, Clemens sidesteps left out of the line of attack. He throws his left arm up and from the inside grabs the wrist of the attacking arm between the dagger and the hand.

3 As soon as he has grabbed the wrist of the attacking hand, he pushes it downward, turning it outward as if opening a lock. At the same time Clemens shifts his center of gravity out and to the left. He thus continues twisting the opponent's arm until he is forced to release his dagger.

There are many possibilities of playing with the footwork here. When twisting the arm one can also take a step to the left or step back. Both will take the opponent roughly to the ground.

DER MAULSTOSS (The Blow to the Mouth)

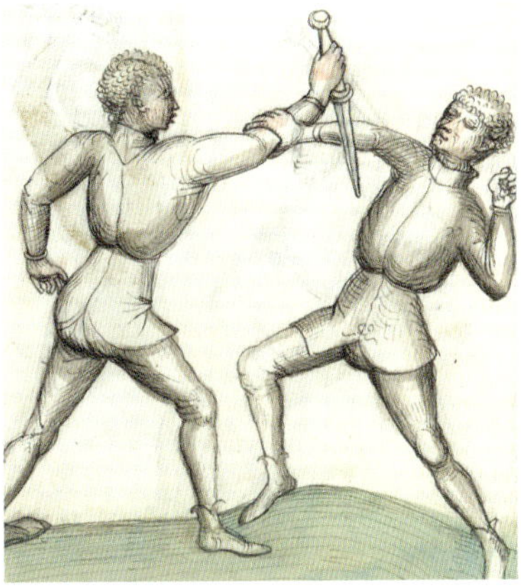

From the KK 5342

"Der hat Im den stich entwert und will Im mit der fawst In das mawl stossen"

1 Clemens attacks out of the From the Roof Guard. Ralf is in the Beginning in Wrestling position and is in a closed stance.

2 If Clemens makes a stab from above, Ralf takes a half step to the left, by shifting his left leg slightly to the left. At the same time, Ralf throws up his right arm and takes the attacking arm.

3 When Ralf has grasped the arm, he pulls on it gently and steps toward the attacker. He pushes the arm out of the way in front of him and strikes the opponent in the face with his fist.

DEN ARM ABBRECHEN (Break the Arm)

1 Ralf is in the Lower Guard and is holding the dagger long. Clemens is in the Beginning in Wrestling position and has an open stance.

2 If Ralf attempts to stab Clemens in the abdomen, Clemens reaches for the wrist of Ralf's attacking arm from the left and right with both hands, while stepping back with his left foot. He thus pulls Ralf's wrist towards him.

3 If Ralf reacts to the pull on his wrist by pulling back, Clemens uses this to step in. Clemens simply allows himself to be pulled and moves his left foot directly in front of Ralf's right foot while raising his gripped arm. He then turns clockwise into the opponent, so that he ends up standing to Ralf's right with his back to him.

4 While Clemens is turning into the attacker, he bends his knees slightly in order to get beneath the arm in his grasp, and brings it onto his left shoulder. When placing the gripped arm on the shoulder, it is important that the elbow comes to rest on the shoulder with the elbow pointing upward.

If Clemens now has the gripped arm on his shoulder, he straightens his legs and pulls the gripped arm to his chest, thus breaking Ralf's arm. If the opponent does not respond to the pull or lose his balance and tumble forward, we simply continue pulling on his arm. We step back further and pull the gripped hand in front of us to the ground. Ralf thus lands on his belly.

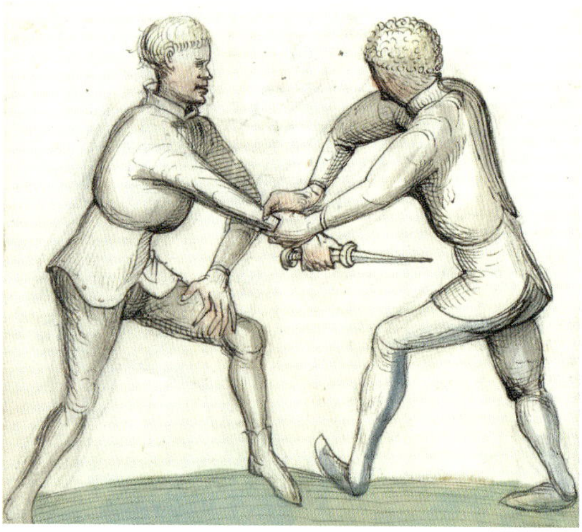

From the KK 5342

"Der hat Im den stich entwert und will Im mit der fawst In das mawl stossen"

1

2

ARM ABBRECHEN, VARIATION
(Break the Arm, Variation)

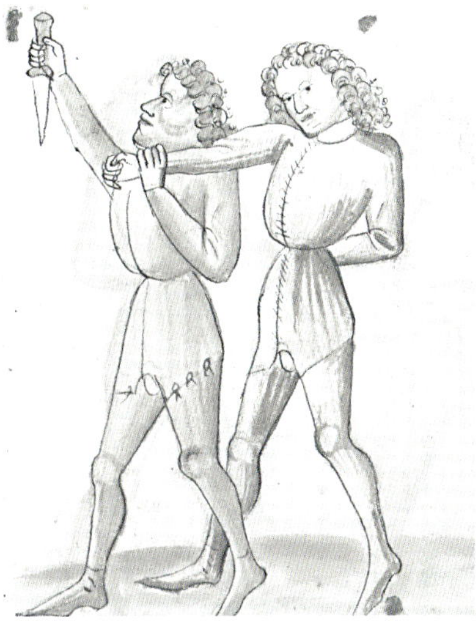

From the Ms. Chart. A 558

This is a variation of the Breaking of the Arm from the Ms. Chart A558. The technique follows the one just described.

After Clemens has stood up and broke the opponent's arm or at least caused him considerable pain, he grabs the dagger, which the opponent can only grip loosely because of the pain. Having captured the dagger, he stabs at the attacker behind his back.

2

3

4

5

6

AN DEN RÜCKEN WERFEN (Throw onto the Back)

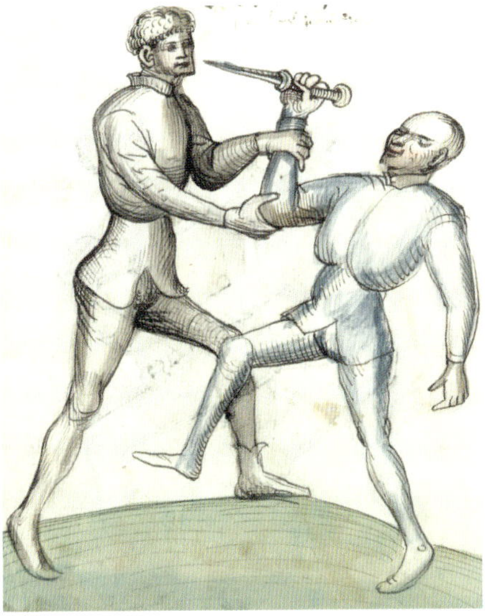

From the KK 5342

"Das werffen an den ruggen und das arm brechen"

1

2

1 Clemens assumes the From the Roof Guard and makes a stab from above. As defender, Ralf is in the Beginning in Wrestling position and is in a closed stance.

2 When Clemens comes down with the stab, Ralf counters by stepping forward slightly with his left foot. He intercepts the stab with his left hand.

3 As soon as the attack is stopped, Ralf reaches under Clemens's gripped arm with his right hand and grasps his elbow.

4 Ralf now steps further forward with his left foot, pulling Clemens' elbow towards him and pushing his wrist downwards, in the direction of his back.

5 6 Depending on how energetically the technique is carried out, the attacker is thrown onto his back or his arm is broken.

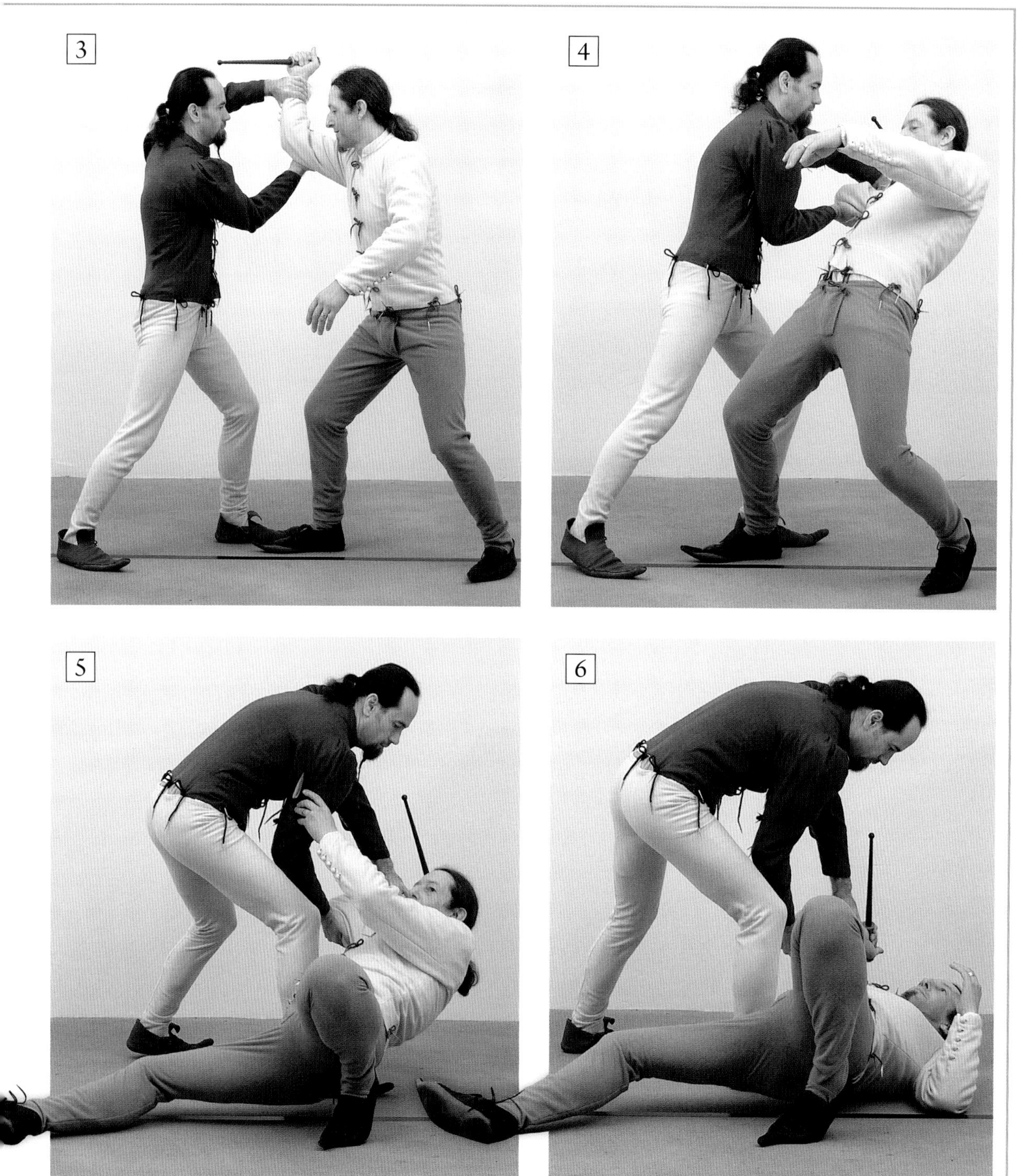
3
4
5
6

MIT BEIDEN HÄNDEN (With Both Hands)

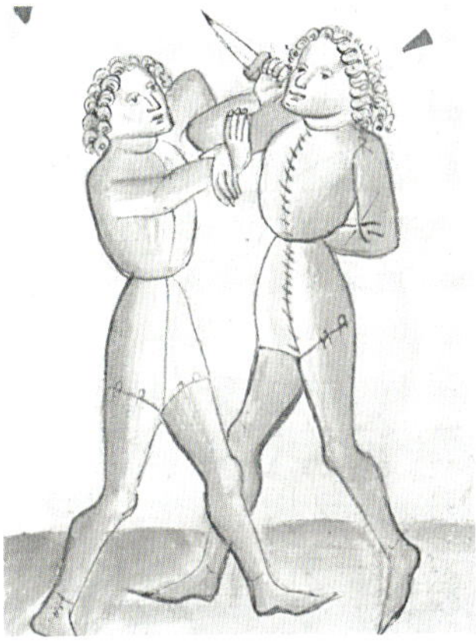

From the Ms. Chart. A 558

1

2

3

1 Ralf is in the From the Roof Guard; Clemens is in the Beginning in Wrestling position in a closed stance.

2 When the attacker's stab comes down, the defender throws up his right arm, stepping his left foot forward, and to the left. With his raised arm he captures the attacking arm from the outside above the elbow.

3 While Clemens now steps toward Ralf with his right foot, he pushes the gripped arm in front of him, moving it upward. As he does so, he passes his free hand from the left through Ralf's bent arm to his right arm, grabbing his own right wrist.

4 When he has grasped his own wrist, he pushes the opponent's captured arm downward.

5 6 He backs up this move by stepping past Ralf's right leg with his right leg, so as to throw him while executing the lever.

Note: Clemens could kick behind the right leg of Ralf with his right leg, in order to throw him off balance.

4

5

6

DER KONTER (The Counter)

From the Ms. Chart. A 558

1 2 3 This technique follows the one just described. We begin at the moment in which Clemens has gripped his right wrist and is about to work past Ralf on the right. This is the latest moment in which Ralf must take action to escape the lever.

4 5 To do this, Ralf simply brings the ball of the thumb of his free left hand under Clemens' chin and pushes his head backward. Clemens is thus forced to abandon the lever.

This break works against all similar levers, in which the one carrying them out steps very close to the one being gripped.

4

5

DER ARMBRUCH (The Arm Break)

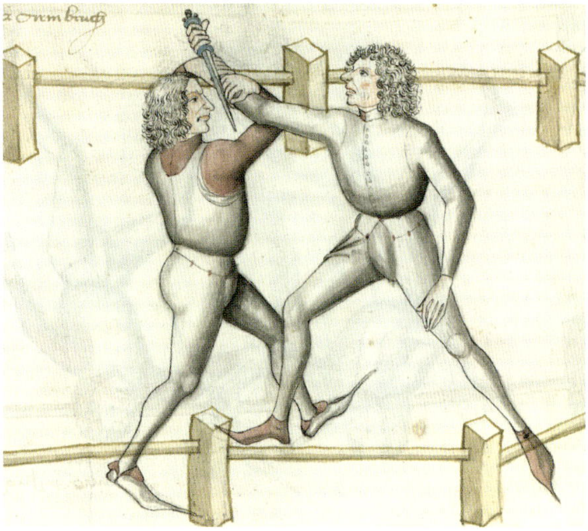

"Der arm bruch"

1 Clemens is in the From the Roof Guard and makes a stab from above. Ralf is in the Beginning in Wrestling position in a closed stance.

2 When Clemens comes from above with his stab, Ralf counters the attack by moving his left foot forward and left. He throws up his left arm, to seize the attacking hand from the inside at the wrist.

3 With his right hand, Ralf reaches through under Clemens' arm to his elbow and grips it.

4 5 While Ralf now pushes Clemens's wrist backward, he pulls the gripped elbow towards him and steps right past Clemens.

6 Depending on the intensity of the lever, we throw the opponent onto his back or break his arm.

1

2

3

4

5

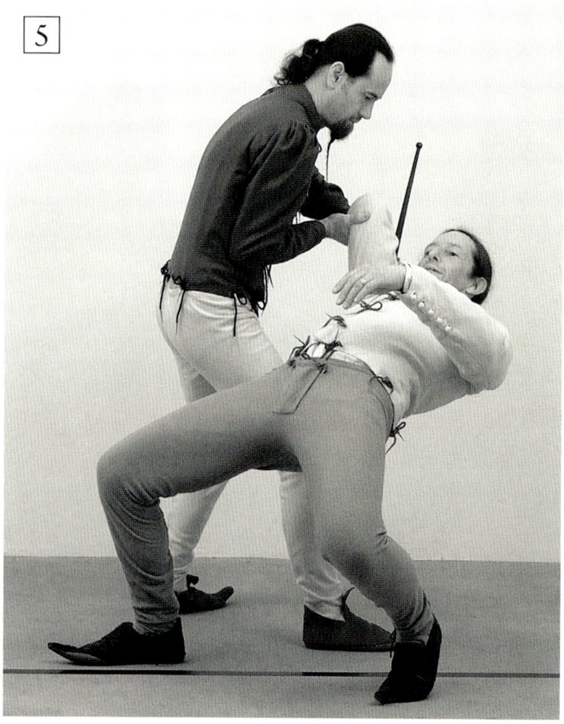

6

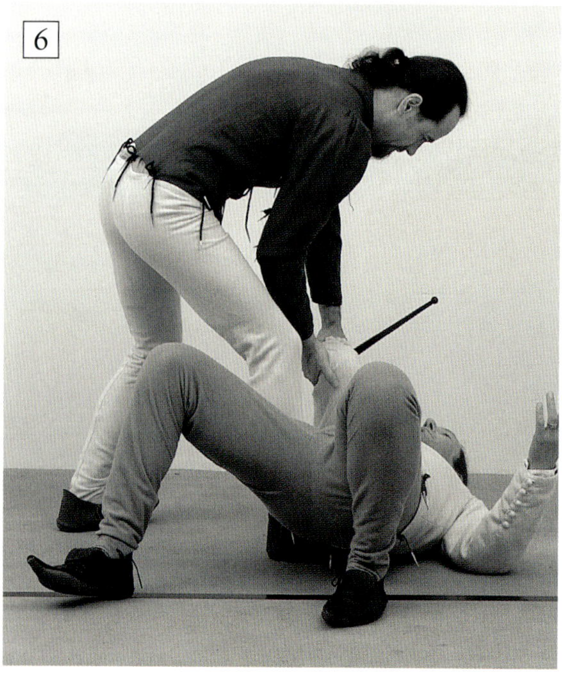

WERFEN MIT DEM DOLCH
(Throw with the Dagger)

1 Ralf is in the From the Roof Guard. Clemens is in the Beginning in Wrestling position in a closed stance.

2 When Ralf delivers his stab from the From the Roof Guard, Clemens steps into the attack with his left foot, so that he ends up standing next to Ralf's right foot. As he does this, he throws up his right arm to capture Ralf's attacking weapon arm from the outside at the wrist.

3 While Clemens, now standing next to Ralf, turns clockwise about his own axis, he guides the gripped arm towards his abdomen in such a way that the elbow ends up on his abdomen with the elbow pointing away from it.

4 Clemens continues turning about his own axis by shifting his back foot to the rear and bending forward slightly. This literally hurls the opponent away if he wants to avoid having his arm broken.

5 Clemens really doesn't need his left arm to execute this technique. So here Clemens uses it to hold Ralf's head further away from him. This limits Ralf's ability to counter and also increases the tension on his gripped arm.

From the KK 5342

"Das werffen Im tegen"

4

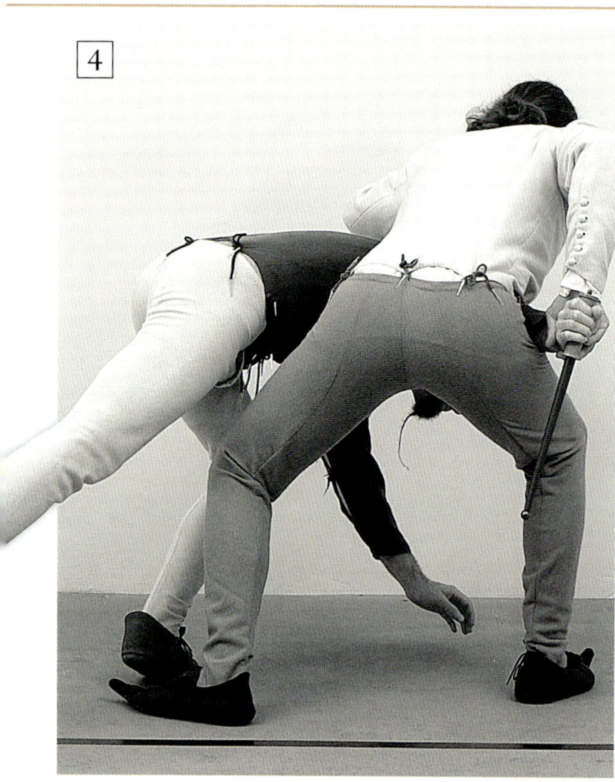

5

DEN MANN WERFEN (Throw the Man)

1 Clemens makes a stab from the From the Roof Guard. Ralf, in the Beginning in Wrestling position in a closed stance, awaits Clemens' attack.

2 When Clemens' stab comes down, Ralf steps his left foot forward and to the left and throws up both arms to block Clemens' stab.

3 As soon as he has stopped the energy of the attack with his forearms, Ralf steps forward and places his left foot inside next to Ralf's right foot. As he does this, Ralf brings both his arms over Clemens' weapon arm and thus pulls the arm close to him. Ralf's right hand reaches for the inside of the attacker's forearm. Ralf places his left arm over Clemens' weapon arm and with it pushes in the direction of the opponent's head. Ralf thus creates pressure on the elbow joint. Clemens is forced backward, making it difficult for him to respond to the lever.

4 If Ralf has now grasped Clemens in this way, he takes a big step with his right foot back and to the right, thus turning about his own axis. While turning, Ralf slides his right hand further down from its grip on the opponent's forearm, so that he ends up grasping Clemens' wrist at the artery. Clemens must follow him and is thrown. If Clemens tries to resist, his wrist is broken.

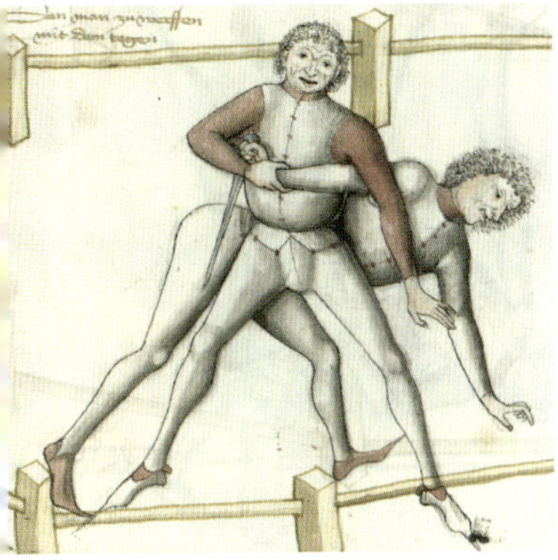

For the Thott 290 2°

"Den man zu werffen mit dem tegen"

DAS RAUFDREHEN (Turn Upon)

From the Ms. Chart. A 558

1

The technique comes from the Ms. Chart A558 and is one of Master Talhoffer's few techniques in which the explanation covers three illustrations.

1 Ralf comes from the Lower Guard with a stab to the abdomen. Clemens is in the Beginning in Wrestling position and is in an open stance.

2 When the stab comes, Clemens steps his left foot forward or acts on the spot, depending on the distance between the fighters. As he does so, he moves his left arm down to block Ralf's attacking weapon arm on the inner forearm. Clemens blocks with his forearm in a circular movement as if wanting to swing a bucket at the opponent's attacking arm.

3 Clemens does not just block, however, instead he continues the movement so that he pushes Ralf's weapon arm in front of him. To achieve this, the block must not be executed too forcefully. If one strikes the opponent's arm with too much force it is knocked away and one can no longer guide it. Therefore one must only push it to the side until the tip of the attacker's blade is no longer aimed straight at the defender but instead points alongside him.

4 As soon as Clemens is no longer threatened by Ralf's blade, he begins winding his arm around that of the opponent while lifting Ralf's arm in his grasp ever higher until it ends up on Clemens's left shoulder. Clemens achieves this by taking a step closer to Ralf while wrapping around his arm.

5 As soon as the right arm comes to rest on Clemens's left shoulder, Clemens places his left hand or forearm behind the elbow on the backside of Ralf's forearm. Clemens now exerts pressure with his left hand, bends his knees somewhat and leans forward slightly from the hips. Depending on the speed and intensity, Clemens either puts Ralf on the ground in front of him or breaks his arm.

It is important here that Ralf's elbow is pointing toward the ground at the moment that his arm is lying on Clemens's shoulder.

2
3
4
5

DAS VERKEHRT WERFEN (The Back to Front Throw)

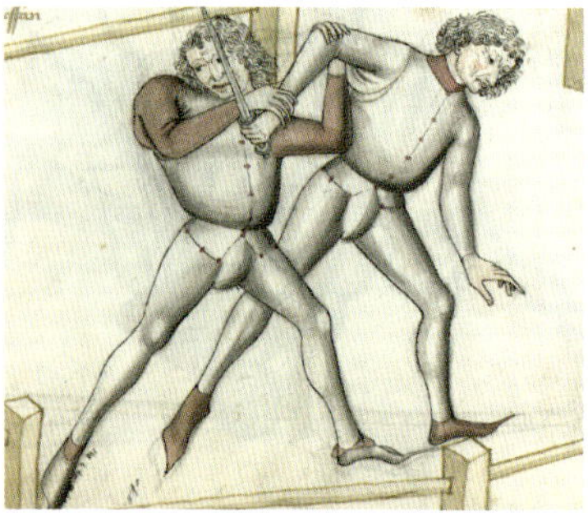

For the Thott 290 2°

"Das verkertt werffen"

1

1 Clemens is in the From the Roof Guard and delivers a stab from above. Ralf is in the Beginning in Wrestling position in a closed stance.

2 When Clemens makes the stab from above, Ralf steps his left foot to the left, out of the line of attack. In the process he throws up his right arm to capture Clemens' weapon hand from the outside.

3 To do this Ralf first halts the stab with his forearm and then reaches for Clemens' wrist with his right hand.

4 He them immediately steps his left foot forward, places his left hand under the bent elbow of the grasped arm and pushes it up and forward.

5 If Ralf now continues exerting pressure in a straight line while stepping forward and pushing the opponent's captured arm over his extended left leg, he simply throws Clemens before him. Or (as in the photo) Ralf pushes the bent elbow down, pulls the wrist upward and bends down from his lower back.

NOTE: It is important that Clemens elbow is still bent and not extended when Ralf reaches under it.und nicht gestreckt ist.

2

3

4

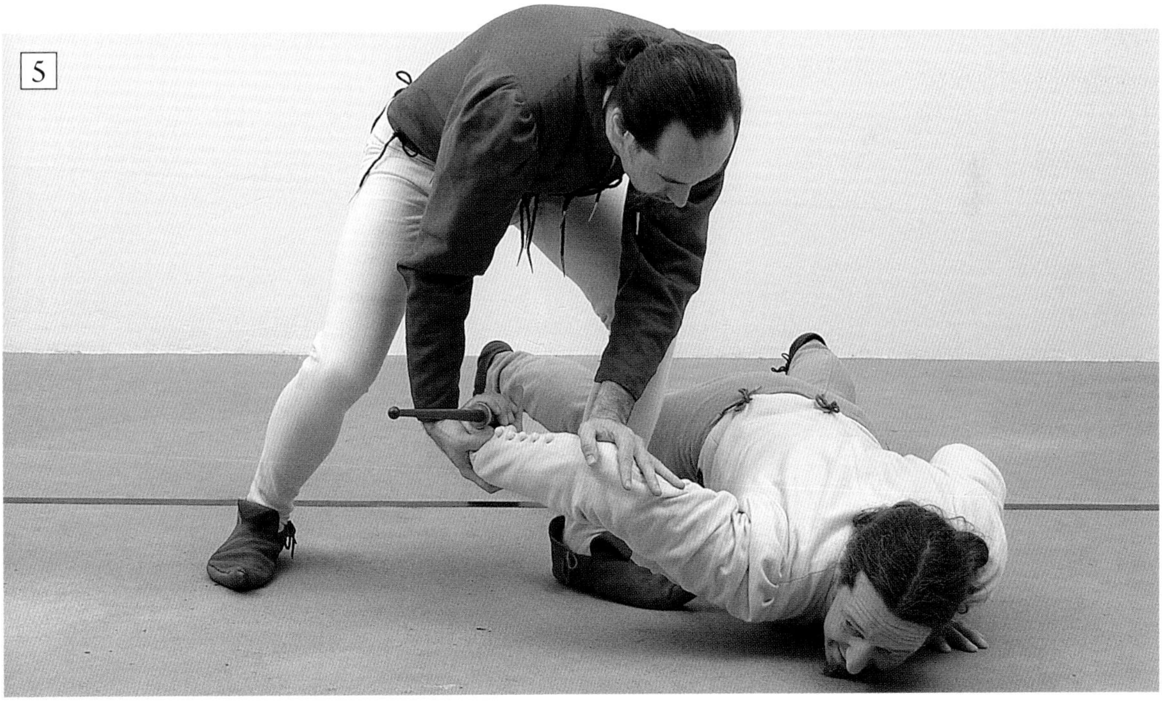
5

DEN DOLCH EINKLAPPEN (Fold the Dagger)

1 Ralf is in the Lower Guard and makes a stab to the abdomen.

2 When the stab comes, Clemens (who is in the Beginning in Wrestling position in a closed stance) takes a small step to the left with his left leg out of the line of attack. As he does so, he turns his upper body to the right, parallel to Ralf's arm, so that he brings his left arm to Ralf's attacking arm and pushes it off line. It is vitally important that one waits until the very last moment to turn outward, otherwise it does not work. The attacker recognizes too soon what one has in mind and corrects his attack accordingly.

3 At this point Clemens' pushing away does not stop the blade, instead he pushes it onward with his left arm by reaching over Ralf's weapon arm. In the same instant that Clemens begins pushing Ralf's blade away with his left arm, he must reach for Ralf's dagger hand with his right hand in order to freeze it. Otherwise Ralf will escape.

4 If Clemens' left arm is past Ralf's, he pulls the captured weapon arm against him, squeezing it between his body and his arm. In this way the dagger is levered out of Ralf's hand.

5 Clemens grasps the dagger in order to stab Ralf with it.

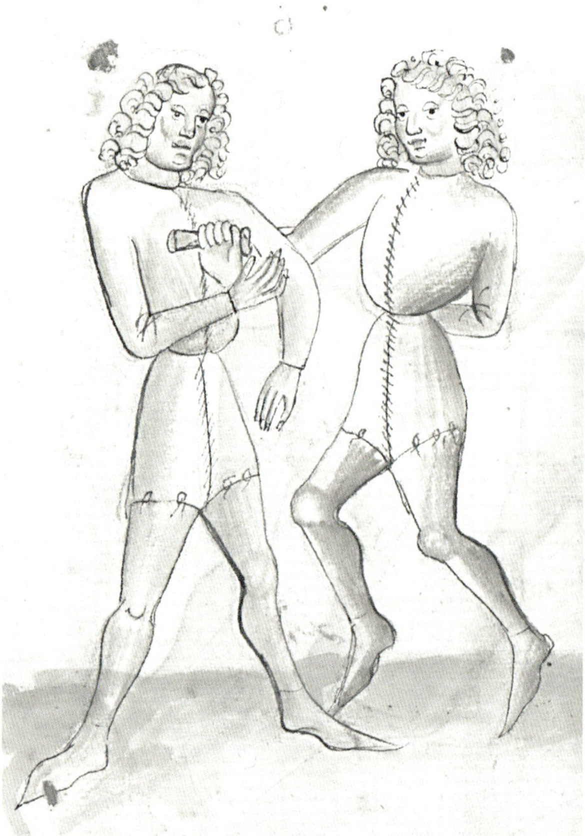

1

2
3
4
5

VON IHM WÜRGEN (Choke from Him)

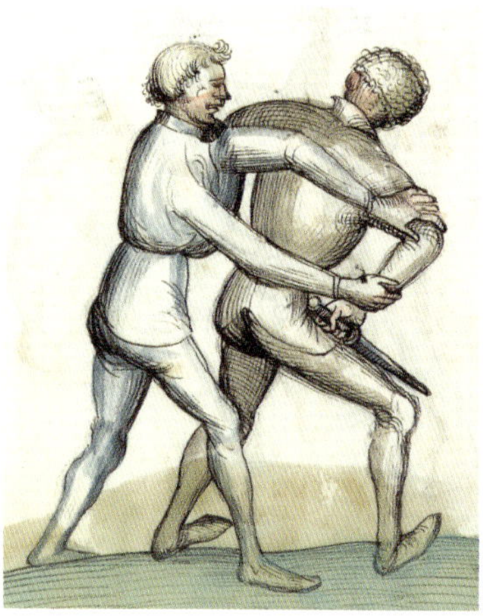

From the KK 5342

"Da hat er Im den stich verseczt und wirgt In von Ihm."

1 Clemens delivers a stab from the From the Roof Guard. Ralf is in the Beginning in Wrestling position in a closed stance.

2 When the stab comes down, Ralf steps his left leg forward to the left, while grasping at the wrist of the attacking weapon arm from the outside with his right hand.

3 Once he has grasped the wrist, Ralf does two things simultaneously: he pulls the wrist down and goes for Clemens' upper arm with his left hand.

4 Ralf does this to freeze Clemens' upper arm while forcing his wrist downward. The gripped arm is bent sharply. Meanwhile Ralf steps behind Clemens.

5 Standing behind him, he pushes Clemens wrist up behind his back and his upper arm forward, stepping forward as he does so. He thus forces Clemens to the ground.

3

4

5

DEN HALS GREIFEN (Grasp the Throat)

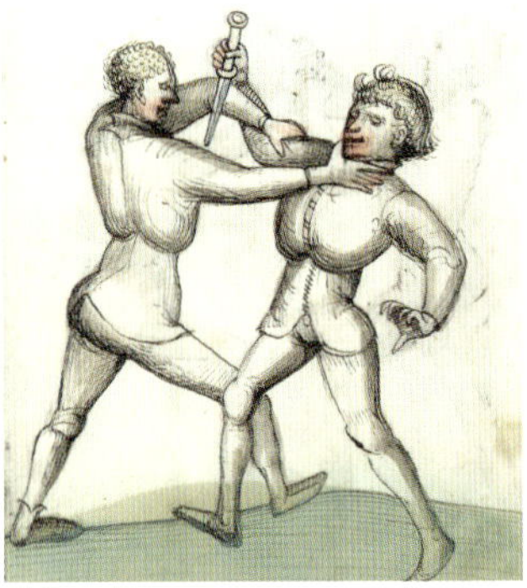

From the KK 5342

"Da hat er im den stich verseczt und (wirgt In von Im – durchstrichen) wirfft In über den füsz"

1 Holding his dagger short, Ralf stabs at Clemens from the From the Roof Guard. Clemens is in the Beginning in Wrestling position in a closed stance.

2 When Ralf stabs from above, Clemens throws up his left arm to parry the move. As he does so, he steps his left foot forward and to the left, out of the line of attack, in order to grasp the attacking arm.

3 Clemens now also moves his right foot forward and places it behind Ralf's right foot. As he steps in, he pushes the weapon arm in his grasp before him and with his open hand reaches for Ralf's throat and grasps it.

4 5 6 To put Ralf on the ground, Clemens pulls his arm outward, exerts pressure on the neck (forcing Ralf backward) and turns his hips to the left. In this way, Clemens throws Ralf over his leg.

In training the grip on the neck is of course done in a friendly manner. In the real thing, however, it is a forceful blow to the neck with the open hand followed by a firm grip.

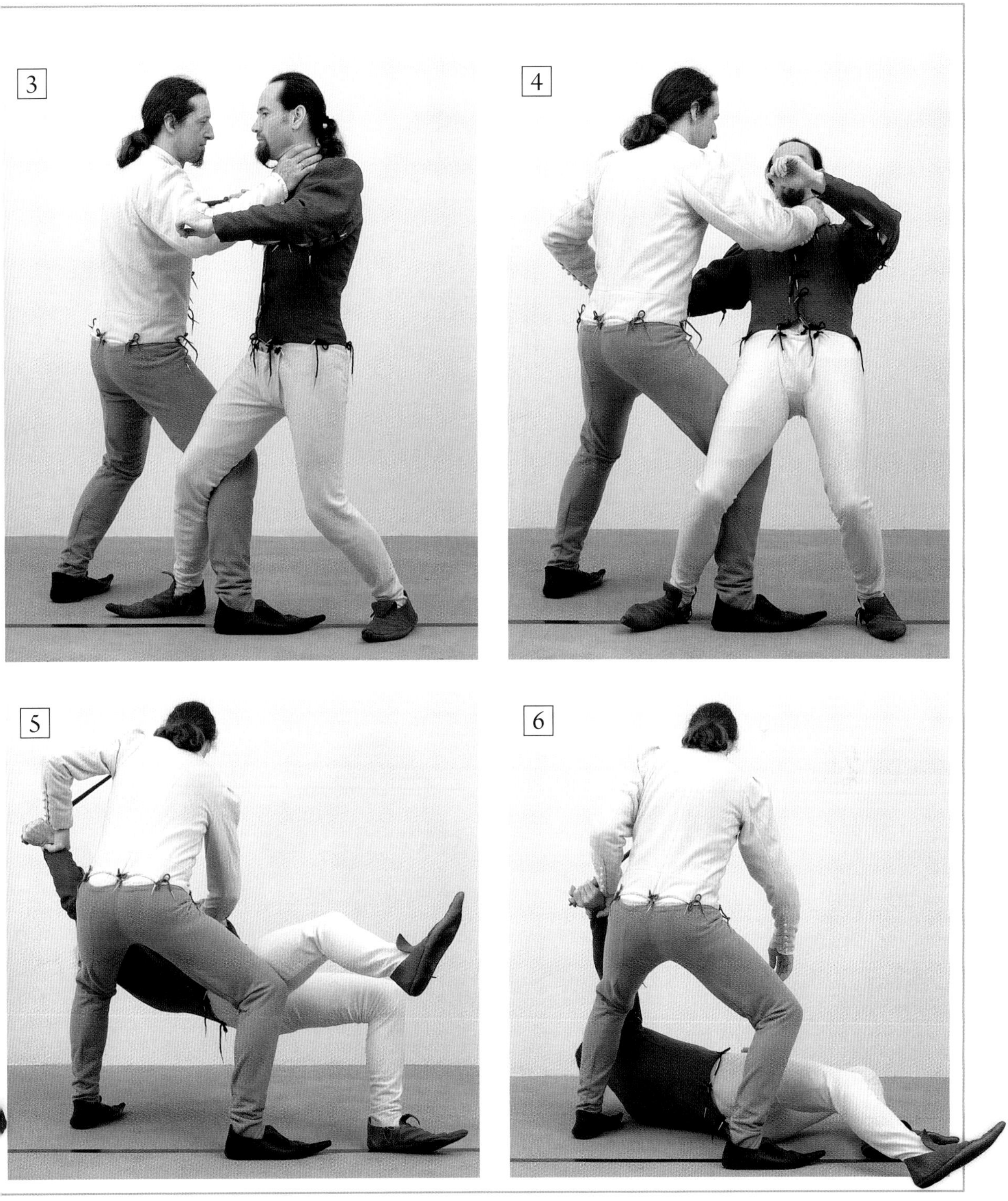
3
4
5
6

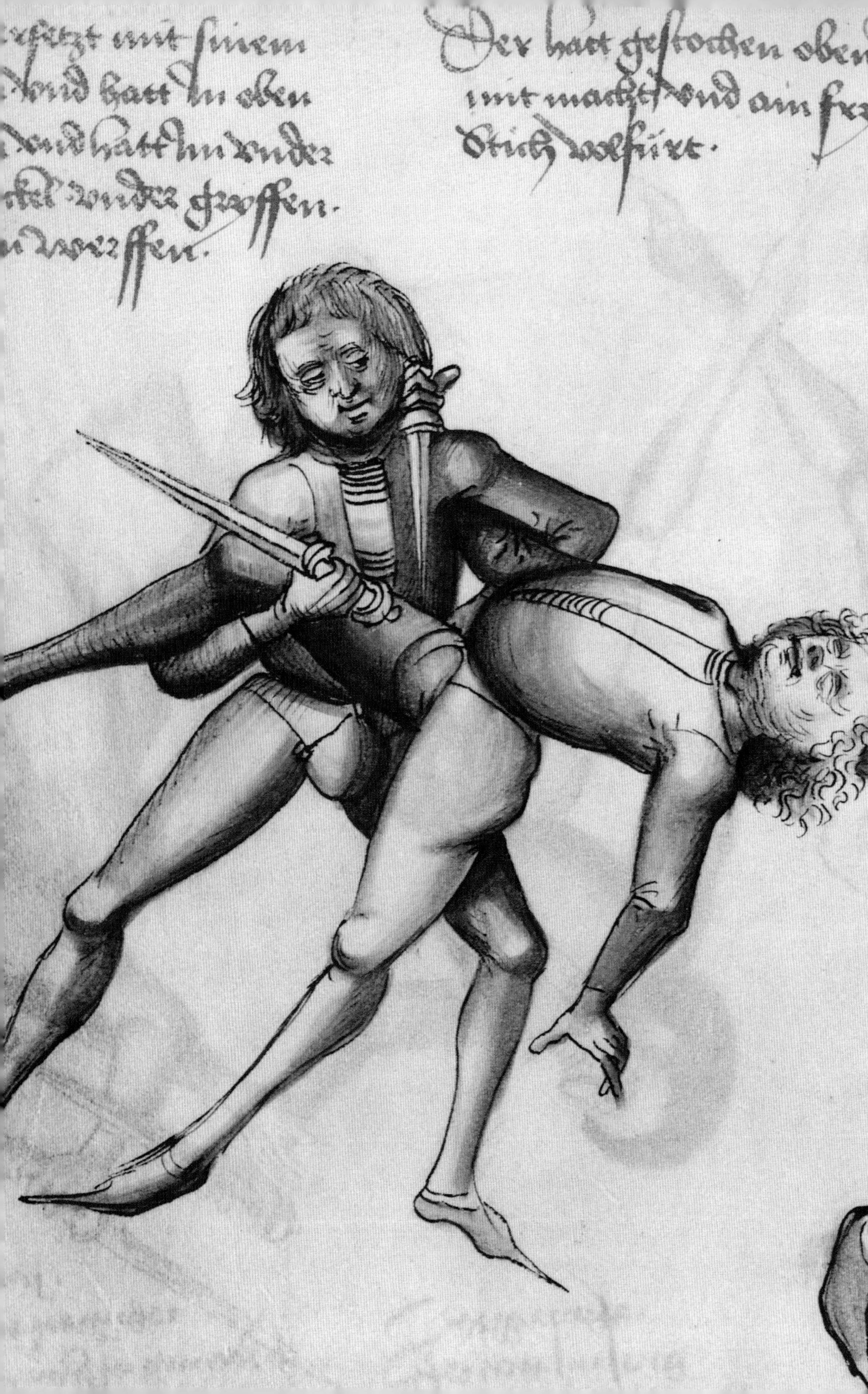

From the Cod. icon. 394a

Chapter 7: Dagger against Dagger

Until now the defender has had no weapon. Now let us turn to the dagger techniques in which both combatants have a dagger. The defender is thus on a par with his opponent.

We begin with the Upper Shield and its set-plays, then come to The Scissors and its set-plays and end the chapter with additional techniques like the Reach-Over, the Arm Break and various throws which cannot be associated with the Upper Shield or Scissors.

In the following techniques, the Upper Shield is used to counter an attack from the From the Roof Guard. We also address techniques that are used to break this Shield. In these techniques it is important for the attacker to let the defender believe for as long as possible that the real threat is a stab From the Roof. Otherwise, the defender will change his parry in time.

DEN DOLCH ENTWINDEN (Twist the Dagger from the Opponent's Grip)

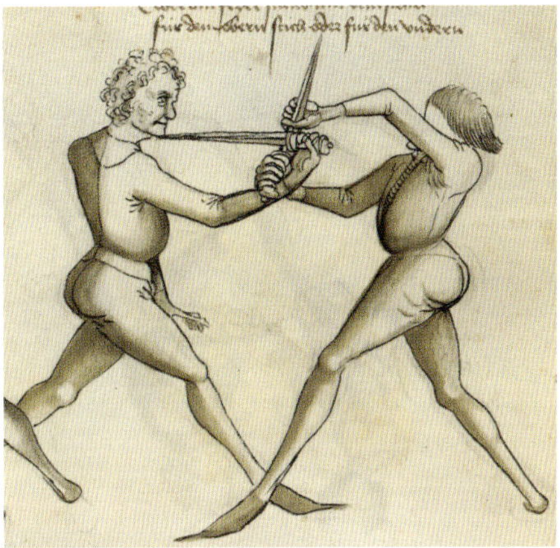

From the Cod. icon. 394a

"Aber ain fryer stand mit den schilt für den obern stich odcr für den undern"

1 Clemens attacks with a stab from the From the Roof Guard.

2 When the stab comes, Ralf takes a step into the attack with his left foot and raises his dagger, that he is holding in both hands, in order to parry the stab with the Shield.

3 As soon as the attack is stopped, Ralf winds the grip of his dagger from right to left behind Clemens' forearm.

4 5 Simultaneously he turns his dagger in front of him, as if turning a steering wheel to the right. As he does so, his blade takes Clemens' with it.

6 He continues this movement until he has twisted the dagger from Clemens's grip.

7 He takes the captured dagger and uses it to stab at Clemens.

NOTE: When in the Upper Shield, one must be absolutely certain that one's face is never directly behind the shield, meaning that the point of the opponent's dagger never points directly at one's face.

The Shield is always executed offset slightly to the right or left—depending on the direction in which it will continue.

Close-Ups Twisting the dagger from the opponent's grip is shown in close-up on Page 106. The Shield blocks the attack. Ralf winds the grip of his dagger behind Clemens' forearm. With his blade he pushes Clemens' blade over his forearm until he is forced to release it.

2

3

4

5

6

7

Close-Ups

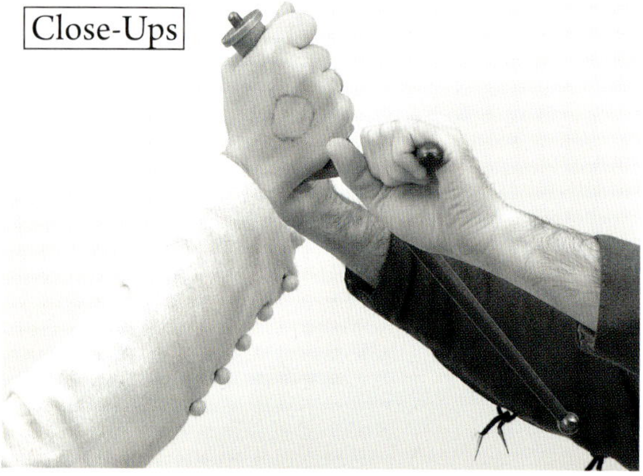

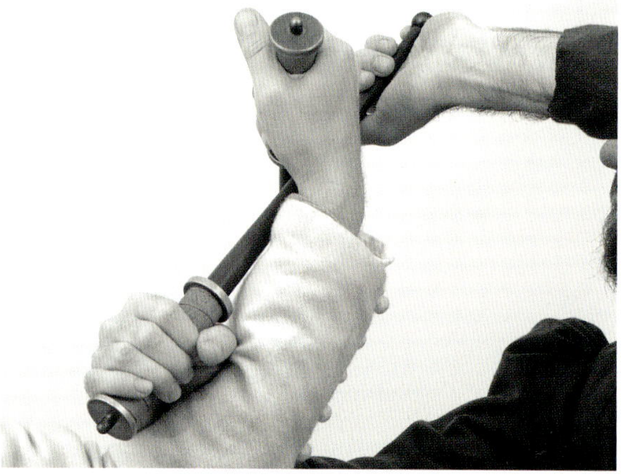

1 This is a variation of the technique just illustrated. Clemens attacks with a stab from the From the Roof Guard. Ralf is in the Free Guard.

2 When the stab comes, Ralf takes a step forward with his right foot and raises his dagger, that he is holding in both hands, to block the stab with the Shield.

3 As soon as the attack is stopped, Ralf places his right foot just behind the attacker's right leg, so that the legs touch. Ralf keeps his leg slightly bent. As he does this, he pushes Clemens' weapon arm in front of him to throw him off balance. Ralf winds his dagger grip from right to left behind the attacker's forearm.

4 Simultaneously, he twists his dagger in front of him, as if turning a steering wheel of a car to the right. He winds the attacker's dagger with the point toward him and thus levers it from his hand. While Ralf is twisting the dagger from Clemens' grip, he continues forcing his weapon arm down and back.

5 If he now suddenly pushes his bent right knee through, it literally shoots into Clemens' right leg. As a result of this and of forcing the weapon arm down and back, Clemens is knocked off his feet and falls backward.

6 Clemens is not thrown in our sequence, however. Instead Ralf takes Clemens' dagger and stabs him with it.

Note: The technique works equally well on the other side, however once the dagger has been wrenched from the opponent's hand it often lands in front of the attacker's feet. He is thus able to pick it up again with his left hand.

DEN DOLCH ENTWINDEN MIT WURF (Twist the Dagger from the Opponent's Grip with Throw)

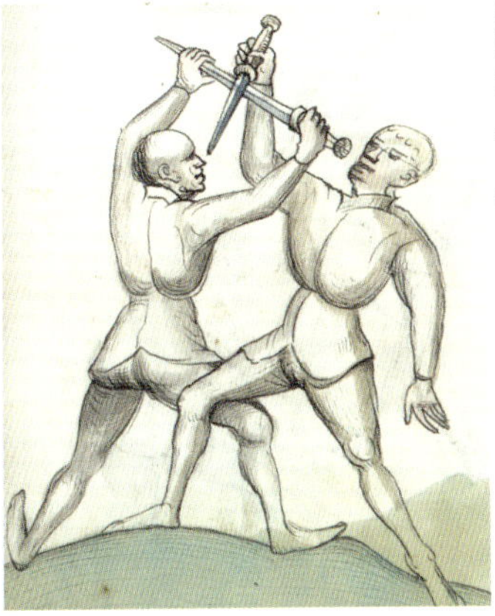

From the KK 5342

"Der ober schilt zu den tegen nemen"

1

2

3

4

5

6

DEN SCHILT BRECHEN (Break the Shield)

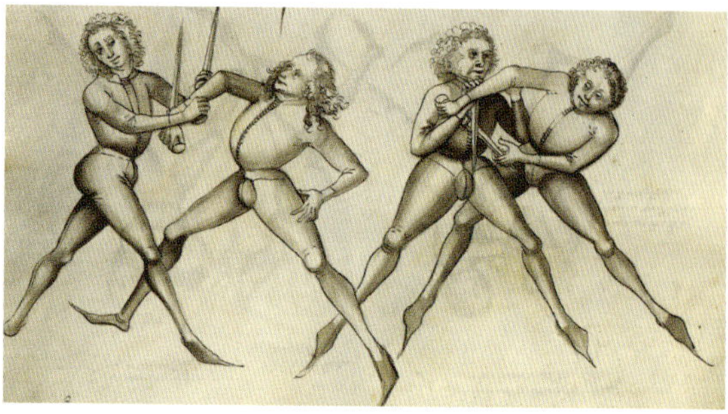

From the Cod. icon. 394a

"Als der den schilt hat gemächt. – So hatt der den obern stich verwent und Stotzt den tegen mit dem hefft zwäschen sinen arm über den schilt und würft In von Im. – Da Verbringt er dasselb Stuck"

1 Clemens begins a stab from the From the Roof Guard. Ralf is in the Free Guard.

2 When the stab comes, Ralf raises his dagger, that he is holding in both hands, in order to block the attack with the Shield.

3 Just before Clemens' stab reaches Ralf's Shield, he changes his attack, leading with the grip instead of the point.

4 With this, Clemens dives through Ralf's Shield between his arms. In the process, Clemens positions his blade against Ralf's.

5 As soon as Clemens dives between Ralf's arms with his grip, he reaches for Ralf's elbow with his left hand and grips it from below.

6 Clemens now places his left foot in front of Ralf and pushes the gripped elbow before him, pushing the arm away, while stepping forward with his left foot. With his blade he pushes Ralf's towards himself, exerting a forward push.

1

3

2

4

5

6

UNTEN EINSCHLEICHEN (Creep In Underneath

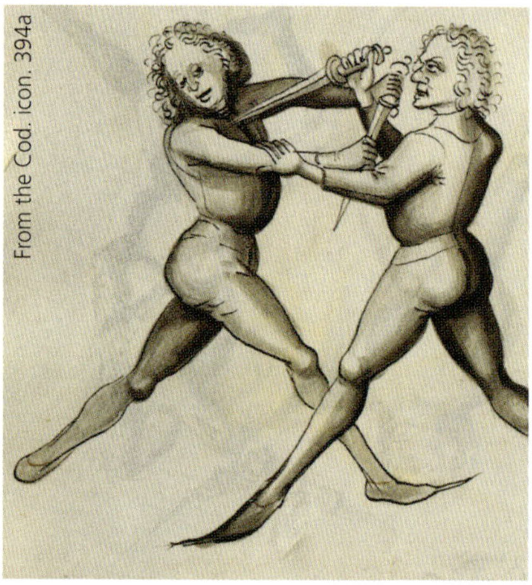

From the Cod. icon. 394a

"Hie ist er uffgangen mit dem Schilt für den obern stich. So hatt der den sich erlogen und slecht unden uff und sticht"

1 Ralf attacks with a stab from the From the Roof Guard. Clemens has assumed the Free Guard.

2 When the stab comes, Clemens steps into the attack with his left foot, and throws up his dagger to execute the Shield and thus check the stab.

3 Ralf modifies his attack, however, and dives through beneath the Shield. He does this by suddenly going to his knees in the midst of the attack, which he has begun from an exaggeratedly high position. As a result, the stab is delivered significantly lower than Clemens expected.

4 While Ralf dives in, he grasps Clemens' left arm with his left hand, preventing Clemens from quickly lowering his arm and thus foiling the stab.

NOTE: It is important not to draw back while stabbing in order to begin again, rather one should simply go lower in a smooth movement. Otherwise the defender will notice the change. When one initiates a stab, one should make as determined an impression as possible.

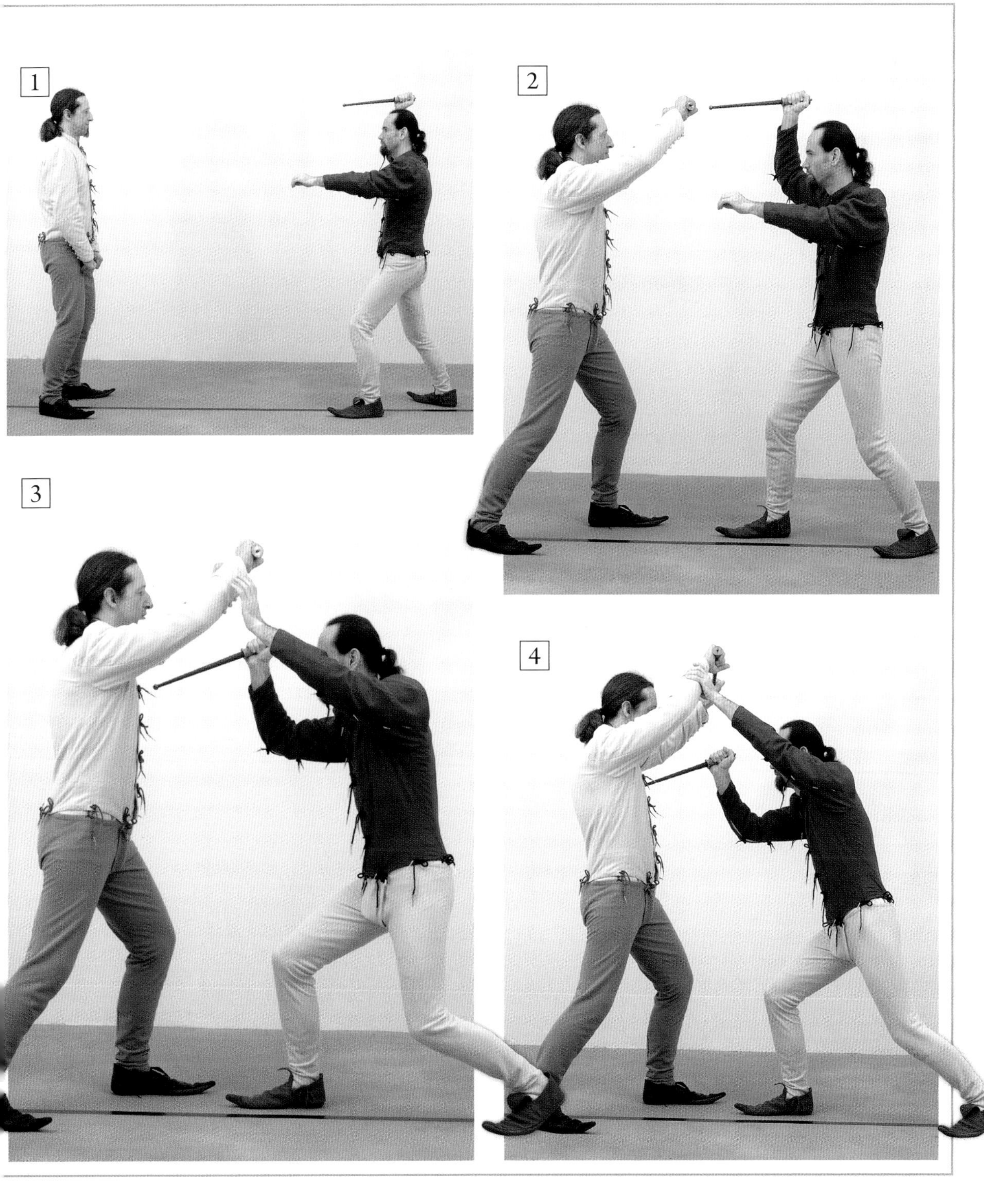
1
2
3
4

DIE ARME ÜBERGREIFEN (Reach Over the Arms)

From the Cod. icon. 394a

"Der hat aber den obern Schild gemächt. So hatt der den sich erlogen und ubergryfft Im bayd Arm und tut In werffen"

1

2

3

1 Clemens comes with a stab from the From the Roof Guard. Ralf is in the Free Guard.

2 When the stab comes, Ralf steps into the attack and raises his dagger into the Shield, that breaks the stab from the Roof. Clemens, however, breaks off his attack by making the step with his right foot clearly shorter than expected.

3 Instead he moves further forward with his left leg and, seizing Ralf's right elbow with his left hand, pushes the opponent's Shield slightly to the right. He is thus in a position to reach around both of Ralf's arms, that form the Shield, with his dagger arm.

4 Clemens does this immediately, once he finds himself beside Ralf's arms.

5 When Clemens has grasped Ralf's arms, he bends his knees in order to grasp Ralf's right thigh from behind with his left hand.

6 **7** Clemens now stretches again, lifting Ralf's right leg and throwing him.

4
5
6
7

DIE SCHÄRE (The Scissors)

From the Cod. icon. 394a

"So hat er In beschlossen mit der schär. – Der hat gestochen ober Inn"

1 Clemens comes with a stab from the From the Roof Guard. Ralf awaits the attack in the Ebich.

2 When Clemens attacks with a downward stab, Ralf takes a step forward with his left foot and stabs after Clemens' attack. Ralf, however, stabs over Clemens' arm behind his dagger, causing forearm to strike forearm. Ralf thus halts the attack and also pushes Clemens' dagger slightly off line.

3 He then brings his own dagger over Clemens' wrist and—reaching through beneath his dagger arm—grips his own blade with his left hand (one must begin moving the left hand as soon as one decides to execute the counter-thrust, otherwise it will take too long).

4 When Ralf has caught Clemens' wrist in the triangle formed by Ralf's crossed arms and the dagger above them, he tightens his grip. This exerts painful pressure on Clemens' forearm.

5 To complete the tactic, Ralf pulls the captured arm down while stepping back.

The location of the attacker's blade when it is captured varies. In the Cod. icon. 394a the opponent's blade is between the defender's arms, whereas in the KK 5342 it is, from the defender's point of view, to the right of his right arm—or outside the triangle formed by the arms.

One thus has two possible ways of initiating the Scissors: one can first deflect the attack to the side with the counter-thrust and then begin the Scissors, meaning that one executes the Scissors beside rather than in front of one. Then, instead of capturing the dagger between one's arms, one takes it outside on one's left forearm. If, however, one takes a step to the right—while moving one's left hand to one's own blade—one captures the dagger between the arms.

One can of course also simply remain standing where one is and capture the dagger between one's arms without first deflecting it to the side. In practice this is rather risky, especially with long daggers. Unfortunately the stab often still finds the mark, though not fully. It is therefore safer to first deflect the thrust a little before beginning the Scissors.

2

3

4

5

SCHÄRE GEGEN SCHÄRE (Scissors against Scissors)

From the Cod. icon. 394a

"Der hat den gefangen usz der schäre. Der bringt dem die Schäre"

This technique is a counter-technique to the Scissors. Simply put, a Scissors is used to break a Scissors.

3 We begin at the point at which Ralf has captured the attacker's dagger hand in the Scissors.

4 With his left hand, Clemens, who finds himself in the Scissors, now reaches for his blade, which is between Ralf's arms pointing downwards, (this technique also works if the defender has intercepted the attack outside his arms). The grip around the blade must be such that the little finger of the left hand points toward the tip.

5 6 As soon as he has grasped the tip of the blade, Clemens squeezes Ralf's forearm with his counter-Scissors, lowers his hands and pulls the opponent towards him.

NOTE: The Scissors employed as a counter is always more effective than the initial Scissors—provided the counter is begun early enough. One must initiate the Counter-Scissors as soon as one is caught in the Scissors. If one hesitates for even a moment, it is too late.

1

2

3

4

5

6

DER BRUCH FÜR DIE SCHÄRE (The Break for the Scissors)

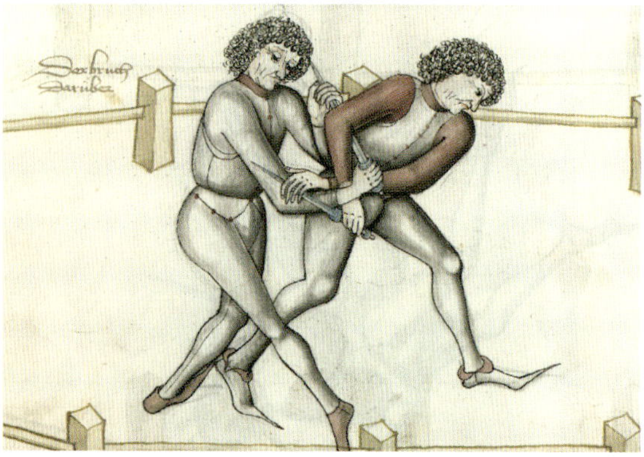

From the Thott 290 2°

"Der bruch darüber"

1 2 3 4 This is also a counter-technique to the Scissors. Here Clemens also grips his own blade.

5 However he changes the grip, so that he is holding the dagger long. The moment when Clemens takes hold of his own blade is the only time that the change of grip can be made without problems. Clemens takes hold of his blade beneath Ralf's arms, lets go of the grip, tilts the dagger to the right with the help of the blade in his grasp, and takes hold of the grip again when he finds himself in the proper position.

It may appear impractical to change the grip on the dagger in the middle of the technique, but in all of Master Talhoffer's manuscripts one can see in the illustrations that he held the dagger short when attacking but suddenly held it long during the break for the Scissors. The break can also be executed much better with the dagger held long.

6 Clemens is now holding his dagger long. He immediately turns his dagger as if wanting to turn right with a steering wheel. The grip goes down and the tip of the blade comes up. Ralf's arms are so twisted that he loses his balance.

7 In the process Clemens steps his left leg in front of Ralf's right leg. He continues turning the dagger towards the ground and assists this movement by turning his upper body slightly to the right.

8 In this way Clemens brings Ralf to the ground in front of him. Executed with more intensity, he literally casts Ralf away from him.

NOTE: When caught in the Scissors, the break only works if one's blade is between the arms of the attacker.

As illustrated in the Cod. icon. 394a, the technique ends differently than in the Thott 290 2°, shown here: in putting Ralf to the ground, Clemens places his left leg in front of Ralf's left and throws him over his leg.

Close-Ups On Page 120 the change of grip once more, this time in close-up. Clemens was caught by Ralf in the Scissors. Clemens now grasps his own blade. He releases the grip in order to push it to the right and then takes hold of the grip again, this time long.

2

3

4

5

6

7

8

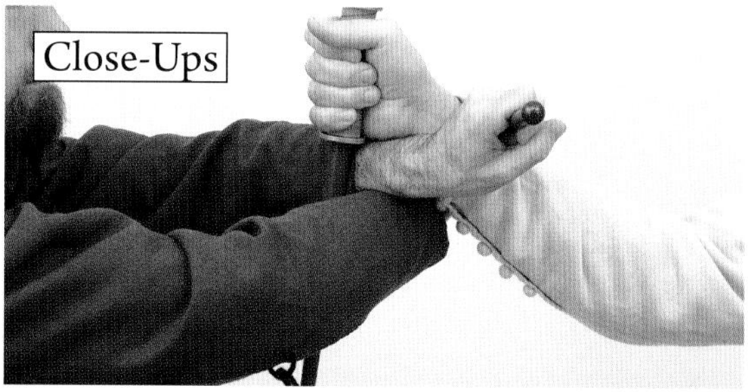
Close-Ups

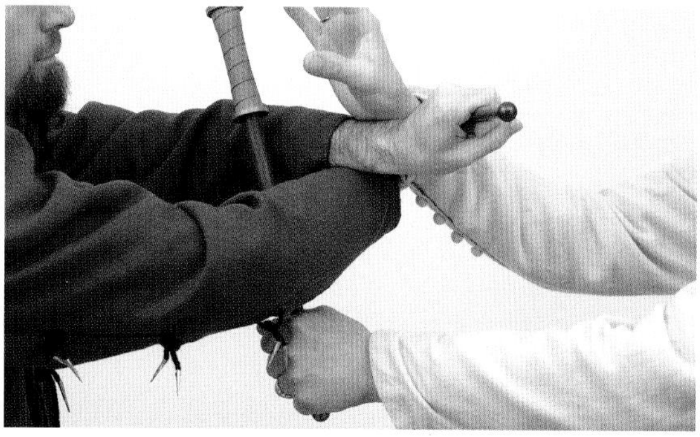

STICH GEGEN DIE SCHÄRE (Stab against the Scissors)

From the Ms. Chart. A 558

2

1

3

A simple, but effective, counter-technique to the Scissors.

3 It begins at the point where Ralf has captured Clemens' dagger hand in the Scissors.

4 5 When Clemens is caught in the Scissors, he switches the dagger to his free left hand and stabs at Ralf—another argument for also practicing wielding the dagger in the left hand.

4

5

DIE HALSSCHERE (The Neck Scissors)

"So hatt och der den beschlossen mit der schäre umb den hals"

1 Clemens has assumed the From the Roof Guard, Ralf the Ebich.

2 If Clemens now makes a descending stab, Ralf steps his left foot forward to the left, so that it is at almost the same level as Clemens.

3 As he steps forward, Ralf throws up his weapon arm in order to place his dagger around Clemens' neck from behind. Ralf lays his blade against Clemens' left carotid artery.

4 Then he reaches in front of Clemens' face with his left hand, over his own and Clemens' arm, and grasps his own blade. As soon as Ralf has gripped his blade, he pulls Clemens to him and exerts pressure on his carotid artery.

NOTE: If we have caught the opponent in the Neck Scissors, we must immediately begin another action to bring the matter to an end. Otherwise he will use the opportunity and stab.

DER HALSSCHÄRENBRUCH (The Neck Scissors Break)

From the Cod. icon. 394a

"So macht der den Bruch und wirt In werffen"

2

1

3

Here is the break to the Neck Scissors.

4 We begin at the point where Ralf has captured Clemens in the Neck Scissors.

5 Clemens now grips his blade with his left hand and now has both hands on the dagger.

6 He pulls the dagger towards him, moving it between Ralf's arms.

7 Then he lunges forward, striking Ralf powerfully in the armpit or the shoulder joint.

4
5
6
7

DER HODENBRUCH (The Testicle Break)

2

1

3

The Testicle Break is another counter-technique to the Neck Scissors.

2 Ralf has gripped Clemens around the neck with the Scissors.

3 To escape this, Clemens simply strikes Ralf in the genitals with the flat of his left hand. This will almost certainly cause Ralf to suddenly ease the pressure of his Neck Scissors.

DAS ÜBERGREIFEN (The Reach-Over)

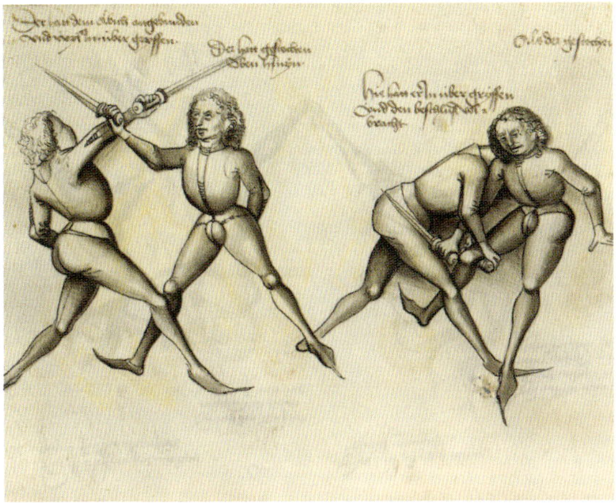

From the Cod. icon. 394a

"Der hatt den äbich angebunden und wyl In übergryffen. Der hatt gestochen Oben hinyn. Hie hatt er In übergryffen und den beschlusz volbracht. Als der gestochen hat"

1 Ralf is standing in the From the Roof Guard and intends to attack Clemens with a downwards stab.

2 Clemens is in the Free Guard and, when the attack comes, steps out to the left with his left foot. As he does so he lets go of the blade with his left hand and throws up his right (weapon) arm, to intercept the stab from Ralf.

3 He does not stop his movement when he reaches Ralf's arm, however, instead he continues it and reaches over Ralf's weapon arm at the level of his upper arm.

4 As he does so, he simultaneously steps his right foot forward, positioning it inside and close to Ralf's right foot.

5 He clamps Ralf's weapon arm under his armpit between torso and arm and then bends his knees slightly. At the same time, from the right he brings his dagger behind Ralf's right leg at the level of the hollow of the knee on the left side. As soon as the blade reappears behind Ralf's leg, Clemens grasps it.

6 He pulls Ralf's captured leg upward and towards him and pushes forward in Ralf's direction with his upper body, which is bent forward from the hips.

7 8 Clemens drives his right shoulder against Ralf's right upper arm, throwing him backwards. Throughout the entire technique, Clemens makes sure that he keeps Ralf's arm squeezed tightly under his armpit.

It is immensely helpful if Clemens keeps Ralf's arm pinned right beneath his armpit and not lower and that this happens as far up Ralf's arm as possible. Otherwise it is impossible for Clemens to have a really secure grip on Ralf's arm. In Master Talhoffer's manuscripts the technique is shown with the dagger held both short and long.

2

3

4

5

6

7

8

DER ARMBRUCH (The Arm Break)

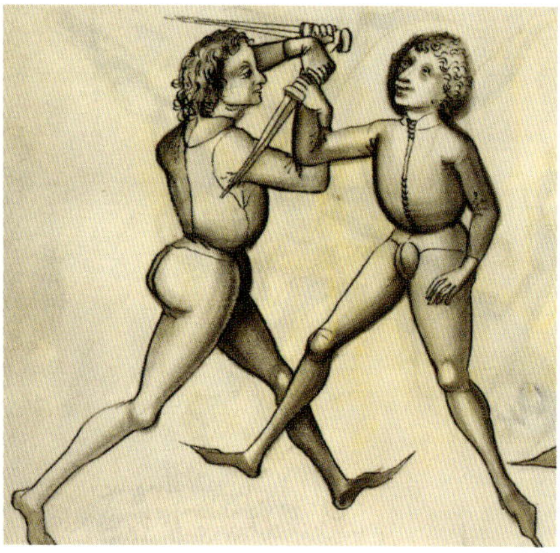

From the Cod. icon. 394a

"Aber für den obern stich ain armbruch und fas sin stich uff den lincken arm und griff mit der rechten hand under sinen arm und zuck an dich"

1 Clemens is in the From the Roof Guard and attacks Ralf with a downward stab.

2 3 Ralf, who has summed the Free Guard, steps forward and out to the left with his left foot. Ralf throws up his left arm and catches Clemens' attacking arm from the inside at the wrist.

4 Ralf takes Clemens' arm with him as he moves left, causing Clemens to open up. By sliding his left foot forward slightly, Ralf can now place his right (weapon) arm around Clemens' upper arm from below and behind. This also brings his weapon hand to Clemens captured forearm.

5 6 7 Ralf now steps past Clemens while pulling the captured weapon arm down in the direction of his abdomen. In this way Ralf breaks Clemens' arm or, if Ralf has applied the technique more gently, forces him to the ground.

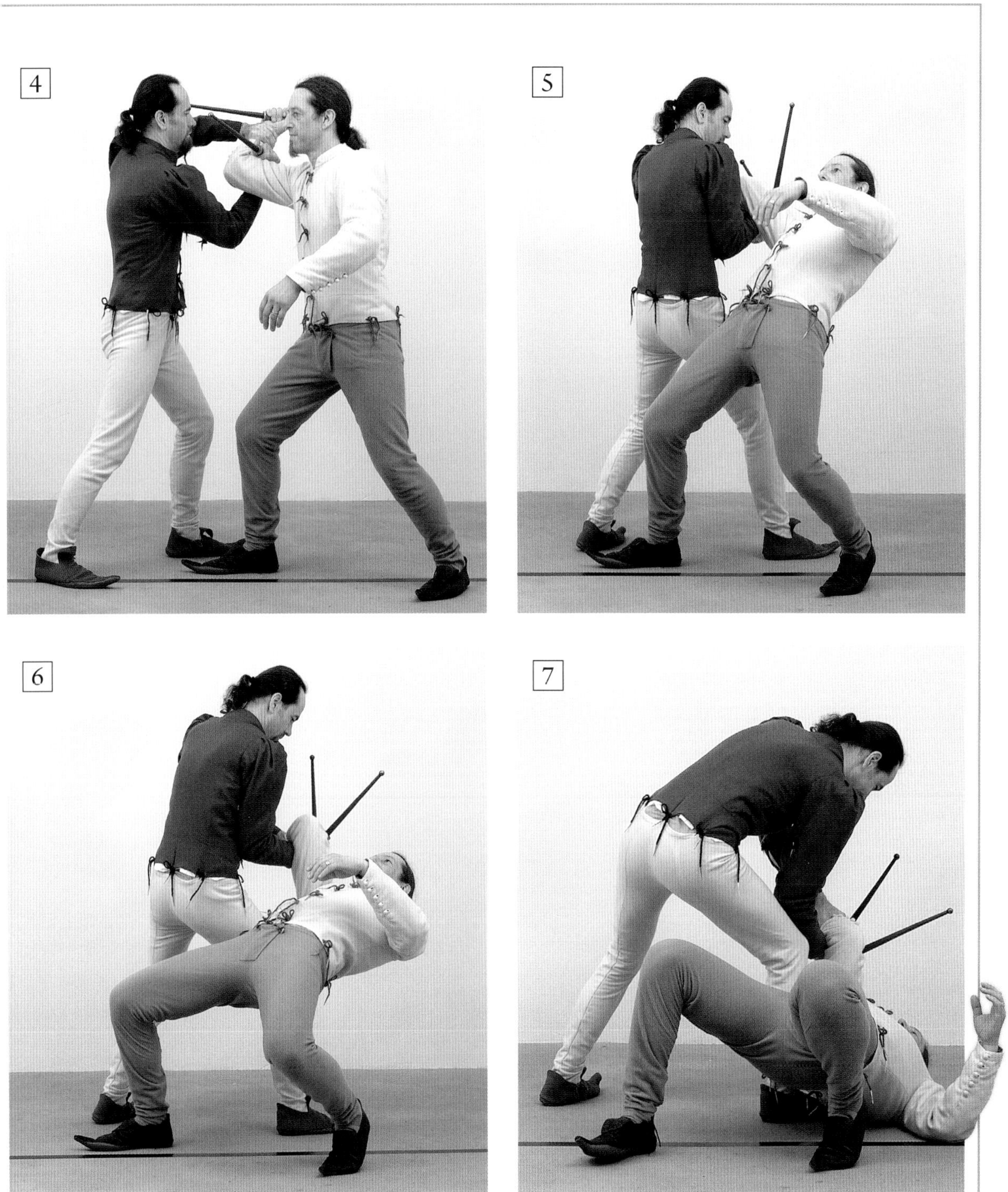
4
5
6
7

DEN ARM ABBRECHEN (Break the Arm)

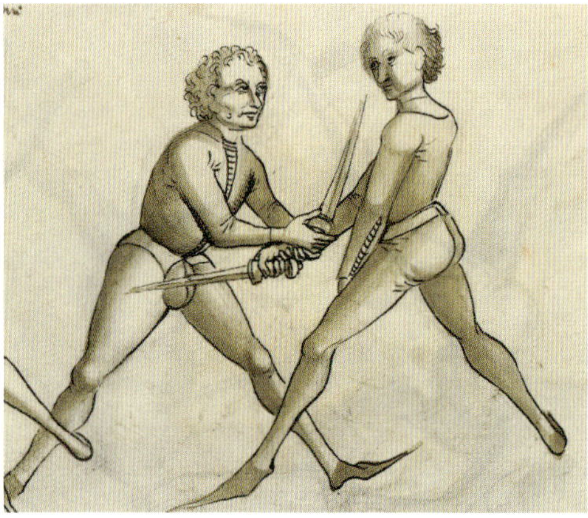

From the Cod. icon. 394a

"Für den undern stich fach sin stich In din bayd hend und wirf Im Sin arm uff die lincken Achsel und brich In ab. Hie ist der armbruch vie vor geshrieben stat"

1 Ralf is in the Zwiffelstich position and from there stabs at Clemens' abdomen. Clemens assumes the From the Roof Guard with dagger held long.

2 When the stab at the abdomen comes, Clemens steps his left foot back, reaches for the attacking weapon arm from the outside with both hands and exerts a pull on it.

3 Clemens uses the countermove to step forward. In order to do this, Clemens pulls Ralf's arm up and to the right —from his point of view—and moves his left foot forward so as to be as close to Ralf's right side as possible. Then he turns clockwise about his own axis into the opponent, with his blade pointing at Ralf's face.

Note: This fact and the situation threatening Ralf, of losing his balance and being pulled to the ground, causes him to reciprocate the pull. Should the attacker, contrary to expectations, not reciprocate the pull, one simply continues to pull him and in this way bring him to the ground in front of one.

4 Clemens places Ralf's captured arm onto his left shoulder, so that Ralf's elbow faces upward and the elbow comes to rest on Clemens' shoulder. During this movement Clemens bends his knees deeply, as this makes it much easier to get under Ralf's arm. As soon as Clemens has positioned himself correctly, he stands up again and pulls Ralf's captured wrist to his chest, thus breaking Ralf's arm.

Note: As the one executing the technique automatically points his blade at the face of the attacker standing behind him when he places his arm on the shoulder, one must exercise great caution when practicing this technique. Proceed very slowly when training in this technique, without masks, and always keep track of the position of your blade tip!

2
3
4

DER WURF AUF DEN KOPF (The Throw onto the Head)

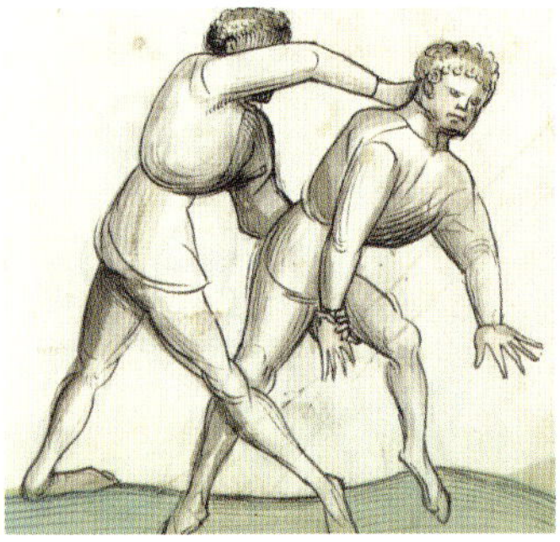

From the KK 5342

"Hie hat er In verkert und wirfft In uff den kopff"

1 Clemens has assumed the From the Roof Guard and attacks Ralf with a stab from above. Ralf is in the Beginning in Wrestling position in an open stance.

2 When the stab comes down, Ralf takes a step forward to the left with his left foot. He raises his right hand and catches Clemens' attacking weapon arm from the outside at the forearm.

3 When Ralf has gripped the arm, he immediately moves his left hand to Clemens' elbow and pushes it upward.

4 Clemens tries to bring his arm down again. Ralf takes advantage of this and pushes Clemens' arm, that he trying to bring down, between his legs towards his crotch. In the process Ralf moves close past Clemens' body, causing him to end up half behind Clemens. Ralf uses his body to help push Clemens' captured arm toward his crotch. There is not much Clemens can do to stop this.

5 If Clemens' weapon arm now appears behind him between his legs, Ralf seizes the wrist with his left hand and lets go with his right hand. Ralf now places his free right hand on the nape of Clemens' neck and throws him onto his face.

6 To do this, Ralf steps his right foot forward while with his left hand he pulls Clemens' captured right hand upward with him and pushes down with his right hand on the nape of Clemens' neck. This throws Clemens onto his face very roughly. Clemens can only avoid this by making a forward roll.

3

4

5

6

DER WÜRF ÜBER DEN RÜCKEN (The Throw over the Back)

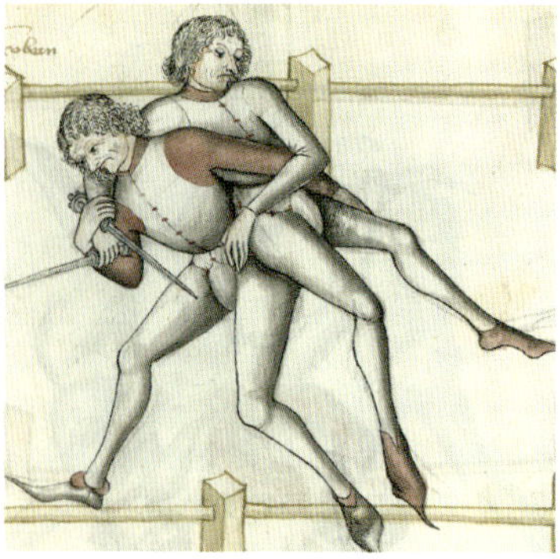

From the Thott 290 2°

"Der wurff ubern ruggen"

1 Clemens and Ralf have both assumed the From the Roof Guard.

2 Ralf attacks Clemens with a stab from above aimed at his right side. Clemens counters this by taking a step forward and to the left with his left foot. As he does this, he grabs Ralf's wrist from the inside with his left hand.

3 Clemens does not pause, but instead continues pushing forward. He steps his right foot to Ralf's right side, beside or behind him, pushing Ralf's captured arm before him, in order to open his stance.

4 As soon as Clemens has moved his right foot, he passes his dagger through under Ralf's arm. He brings his dagger from behind under Ralf's arm at wrist level.

5 Clemens' right hand now takes control of Ralf's weapon arm, holding it captured between his own forearm and the blade. This leaves Clemens' left hand free.

6 Clemens now turns about his own axis counterclockwise, until he is standing parallel to Ralf. In doing so Clemens positions his left foot centrally behind Ralf's legs and places his hip close to Ralf's. Clemens now wants to reach around Ralf's abdomen in order to grasp him behind his left thigh. Clemens strikes him in the abdomen with his left elbow, in order to prevent him from countering and to "soften" him up. Simultaneously he turns into Ralf and reaches around him with his left arm. The elbow blow should not be too hard, just powerful enough to cause Ralf to wince. If the blow is too powerful Ralf will bend far forward, which would rather hinder the subsequent execution of the throw.

7 When Clemens seizes Ralf's leg (if the opponent is wearing loose trousers, one can also grip these), he bends his knees and brings his hip under Ralf's (it is vital that one places one's hip under that of the opponent, for if the technique is not correct at this point the throw will not work).

8 Clemens rams his hip under that of Ralf, pulls the captured leg up and pulls the gripped arm to the right.

9 **10** **11** While Clemens comes back up and twists to the left at the hips while bending forward, he throws Ralf over his back.

2

3

4

5

6

7

8

9

10

Close-Up

Taking control of the opponent's weapon in close-up. Clemens clamps Ralf's weapon arm between his forearm and his dagger.

11

DEN WURF BRECHEN (Break the Throw)

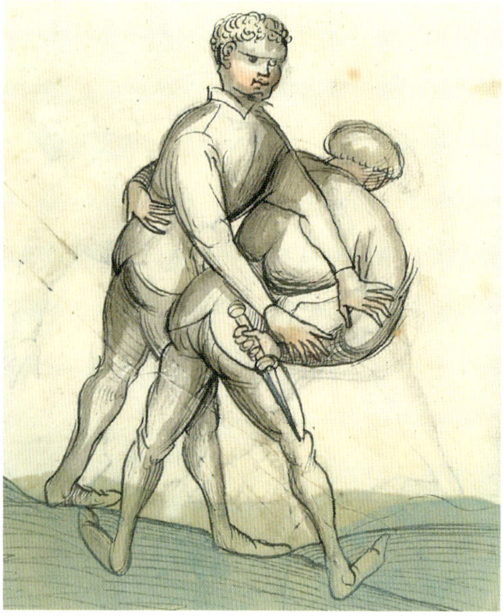

From the KK 5342

"Stuck und bruch"

2

1

3

1 to 6 Ralf can break the just-described throw by letting go of his dagger at the moment that Clemens begins the throw. With both hands he reaches behind Clemens' back, grasps his left upper arm and presses against it. Thus Clemens cannot throw him.

4

5

6

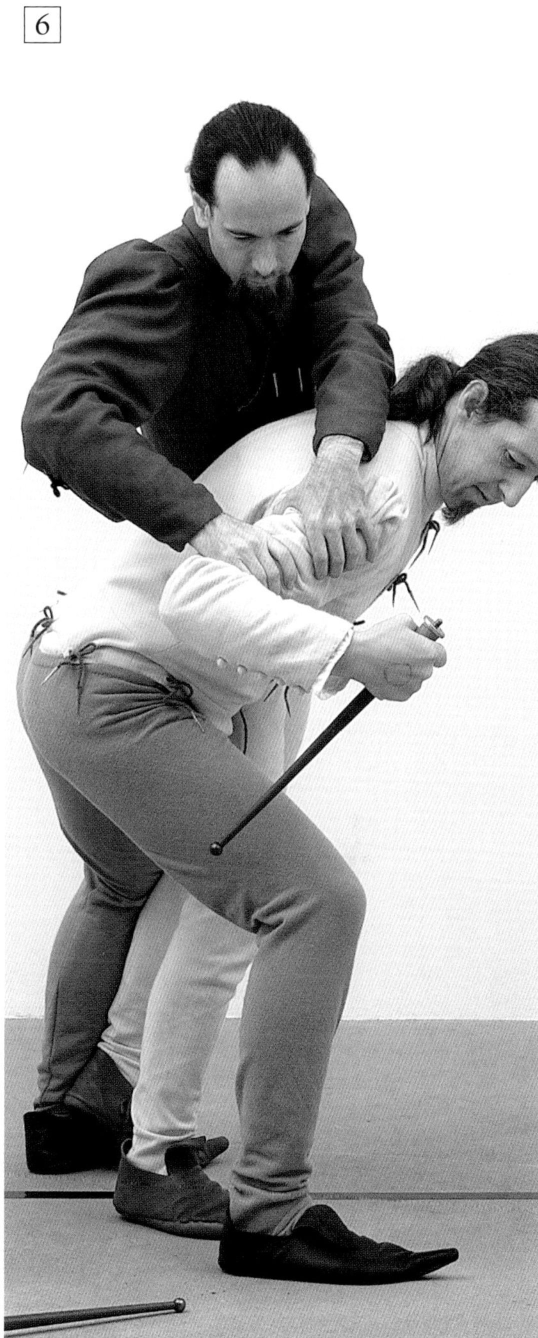

MIT GEWALT WERFEN (Throw Forcefully)

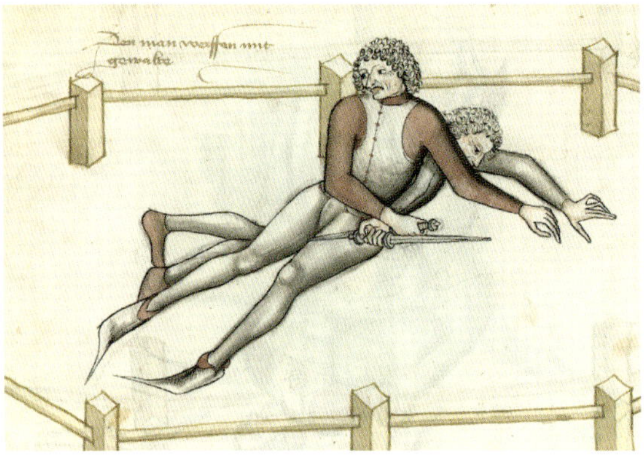

From the Thott 290 2°

"Den man werffen mit gewalte"

1 Ralf is in the From the Roof Guard and makes a stab from above. Clemens is in the Ebich.

2 When the stab comes down, Clemens steps his left foot forward and left. At the same time he raises his right (dagger) arm to intercept Ralf's attacking weapon arm. He stabs against Ralf's stab. The stab is aimed at an imaginary position behind Ralf's wrist and above his arm. When they meet, forearm strikes forearm. In this way Clemens brings his blade over Ralf's forearm, as a result of which Ralf's forearm is between Clemens' blade and his forearm. To hold Ralf's arm, Clemens presses his dagger in the direction of his forearm, so that Ralf's arm—which is between them—is sandwiched (of course Ralf can free himself with enough with enough effort, but the grip is sufficient to hold him briefly and considerably delay his defense).

3 Clemens brings the captured arm further down to his own side and steps his left foot in front of Ralf's right foot. As he does this, Clemens turns clockwise into Ralf.

4 Meanwhile Clemens brings his left arm over Ralf's weapon arm and reaches under Ralf's weapon hand. Clemens now strikes Ralf's upper arm-shoulder area with his back, and he simply throws himself back and pulls Ralf's hand up towards him.

5 If, in the process, Clemens torso strikes against Ralf's upper arm at the end of the rotation movement, this gives Ralf a strong push forward. That and the simultaneous placing of one's own body weight on the upper arm-shoulder area of Ralf, who has been knocked off balance, pulls him over.

6 Thus Ralf is thrown forcefully to the ground—if he reacts smoothly. If not, he will still go to the ground, but his arm will also be broken.

During training, one should approach this technique slowly in the beginning. This is, however, rather difficult, as this technique relies on kinetic energy to function. Not until the training partner can fall safely can one gradually increase the speed of execution. When falling, one should not try to support oneself with one's left arm, as it can be broke relatively easily.

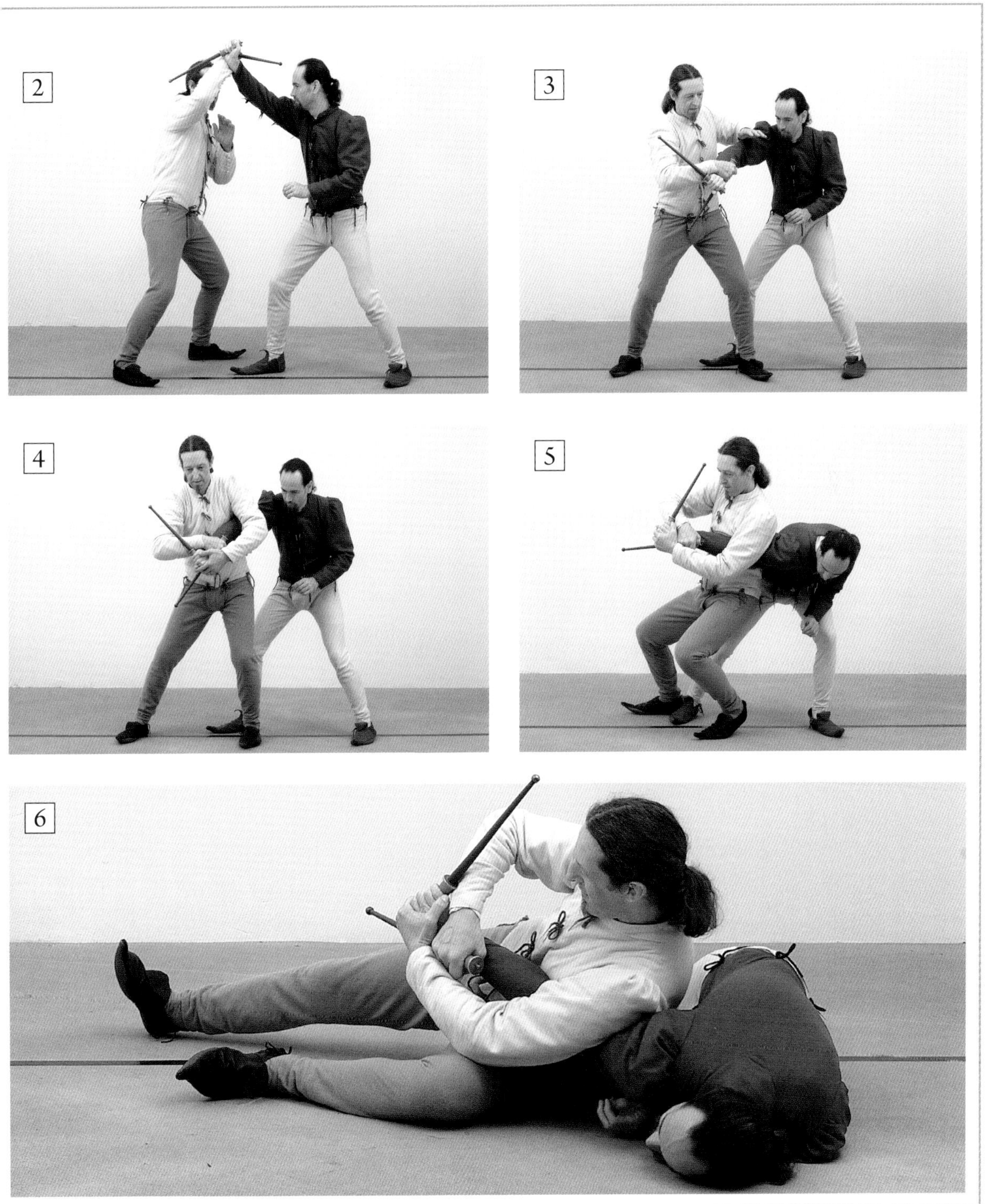
2
3
4
5
6

DER SEITENSTICH (The Side Stab)

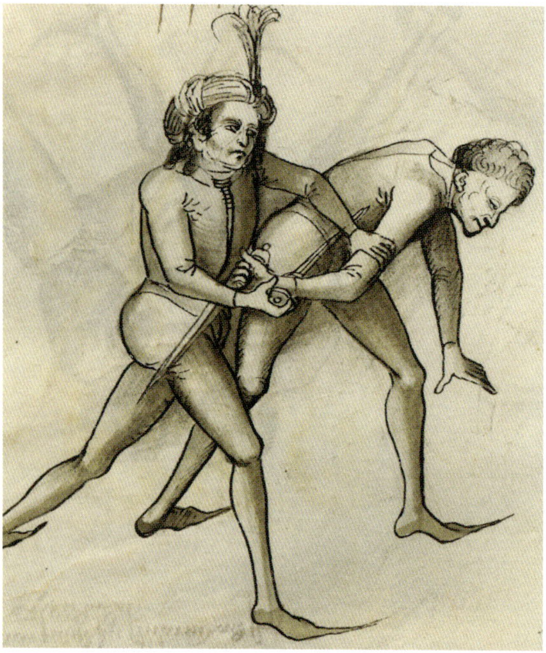

From the Cod. icon. 394a

"Aber für den obern stich würff den Rechten arm uff und fach sin stich daruff und gryff mit den lincken hand In sin Elbogen und truck In von dir für sich Nyder"

1

2

1 Clemens threatens with a stab from the From the Roof Guard. Ralf awaits this in the Ebich.

2 As soon as the stab comes down, Ralf steps forward and to the left with his left foot, so that the outside of his left foot ends up at almost the same level as Clemens' right foot. As he does so, he raises his weapon hand and catches the opponent's weapon arm, in that Ralf again stabs over Clemens' weapon arm and binds it between his forearm and dagger (as described in the last technique "Throw Forcefully").

3 As Ralf's weapon arm is intercepting Clemens' and directing it downward, Ralf moves his left hand forward and in the direction of Clemens' elbow.

4 He pushes it upward, so that on the one hand Ralf's right hand takes Clemens' seized wrist downward and on the other Ralf's left hand brings Clemens' elbow upward. As a result Clemens is put off balance.

5 From the move, Ralf directs a stab at Clemens' right side. Simultaneously he steps his right foot in front of Clemens. While stepping forward, Ralf changes the direction of pressure on Clemens' elbow—no longer upward, but in Clemens' direction of movement, in order to throw him forwards.

3

4

5

DER BRUCH ZUM SEITENSTICH (The Break to the Side Stab)

From the Cod. icon. 394a

"Der bruch ker dich gar umb und würff In über die huffen"

The following is the break for the just-described technique.

2 It begins at the point where Ralf has seized Clemens' weapon hand and placed his left hand on Clemens' elbow.

3 Clemens stands up and raises his right elbow. He tries to control Ralf's dagger hand with his dagger hand.

4 Clemens now takes a big step forward with his right foot to get to Ralf's right side.

5 Once there, Clemens places his left foot behind Ralf's right. As he does so he holds Ralf's weapon arm with his dagger as best he can, or he reaches for his sleeve.

6 If Clemens' left foot is now behind Ralf's right foot, he reaches forward across Ralf's abdomen to the back of his left thigh. As he does so, Clemens elbows Ralf in the abdomen with his elbow as a distraction—but not so firmly, not so hard, that Ralf winces. A blow that is too powerful would cause Ralf to assume a fetal position and thus bend far forward. That would not be favorable for the planned throw.

7 8 9 10 As soon as Clemens grasps Ralf's thigh, he bends his knees deeply in order to drive his hip under Ralf's. Then he stands up, taking Ralf's leg with him as he does, and turns left with a slight movement of the hips. In this way he throws Ralf over his back.

But here is the alpha and omega—as in any hip throw—the driving of one's hip under the opponent's hip. In doing so, we sweep the ground out from under the opponent's feet, so to speak. If this is not executed correctly, the throw will not work.

The formulation *"ker dich gar umb"* in the original text caused us great difficulty. If we simply turned around, we never ended up in a situation that even resembled the one depicted.

Only by caning to the other side could a result be achieved that resembled the depictions by Master Talhoffer.

2

3

4

5

6
7
8
9
10

WURF ÜBER DIE HÜFTE (Throw over the Hip)

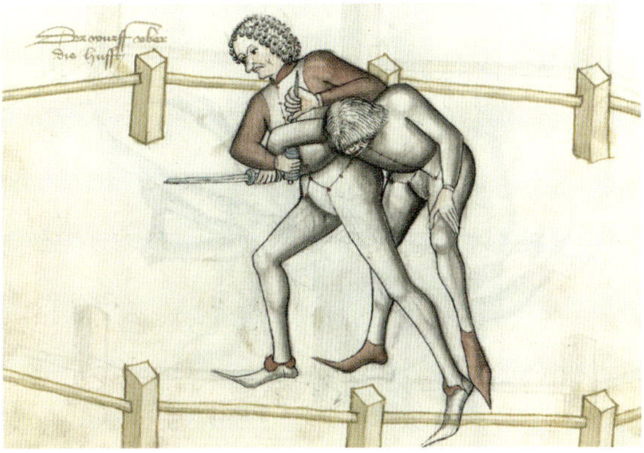

From the Thott 290 2°

"Der wurff über die hüfft"

1 From the From the Roof Guard, Clemens approaches and threatens with a stab from above.

2 When the stab comes, Ralf, who has assumed the Free Guard, moves his left foot slightly to the left. Simultaneously he lets go of the blade with his left hand. He throws up his right arm, which has become his weapon arm, and blocks the stab with his forearm, though not too hard, just firmly enough to stop the attack.

3 4 Ralf now winds his dagger over Clemens' forearm, then again under the upper arm just behind the elbow.

5 He grasps the blade of the dagger, which has reappeared under Clemens's forearm, with his left hand.

6 Ralf now steps his left foot just in front of Clemens, bends forward slightly, pulls his right arm toward him and extends his left.

7 In doing so Ralf continues moving Clemens' arm further downwards and steadily pushes forward. In this way he throws the attacker over his foot. If we execute this technique with our leg very close in front of the opponent's leg, we may possibly break his arm and leg.

4
5
6
7

GROSSER WÜRF (Big Throw)

From the Cod. icon. 394a

"Für den obern stich Ain grosser worff gang mit dem rechten Arm uff und fal mit den lincken arm über sinen rechten arm und würff In von Dir"

1 Ralf comes with a stab from the From the Roof Guard. Clemens is standing in the Zwiffelstich position.

2 When Ralf's stab comes down, Clemens takes his dagger in his left hand and steps his left leg forward to the left, so that he ends up with his left foot very close to the outside of Ralf's right foot. As he does this, he raises both arms to block Ralf's stab.

3 He absorbs the initial energy of the attack with his forearms, in order to then bring both arms over Ralf's weapon arm. He brings his left arm all the way over, so that it ends up pointing at the ground. With his right he reaches under the elbows for Ralf's inner forearm.

4 Clemens now describes a semicircle to the rear with his right foot. He turns clockwise into the attacker as if wanting to stand with his back to him (this does not happen, however, as Ralf is immediately pulled around).

5 While turning, Clemens' right hand moves down Ralf's captured forearm and pulls it towards him. When his turn is completed, he has gripped Ralf's wrist.

Clemens now has two courses of action to choose from: if he remains upright while turning and releases Ralf with his left arm, he throws him away. But if he bends forward—as shown here—Clemens takes Ralf to the ground with him.

Note: It is important that the crook of Ralf's elbow is pointing away from him, the elbow toward him and that Clemens presses Ralf's right hand against his body. His turn and the resulting pressure on Ralf's upper arm produce an elbow lever. With sufficient intensity, Clemens breaks Ralf's elbow.

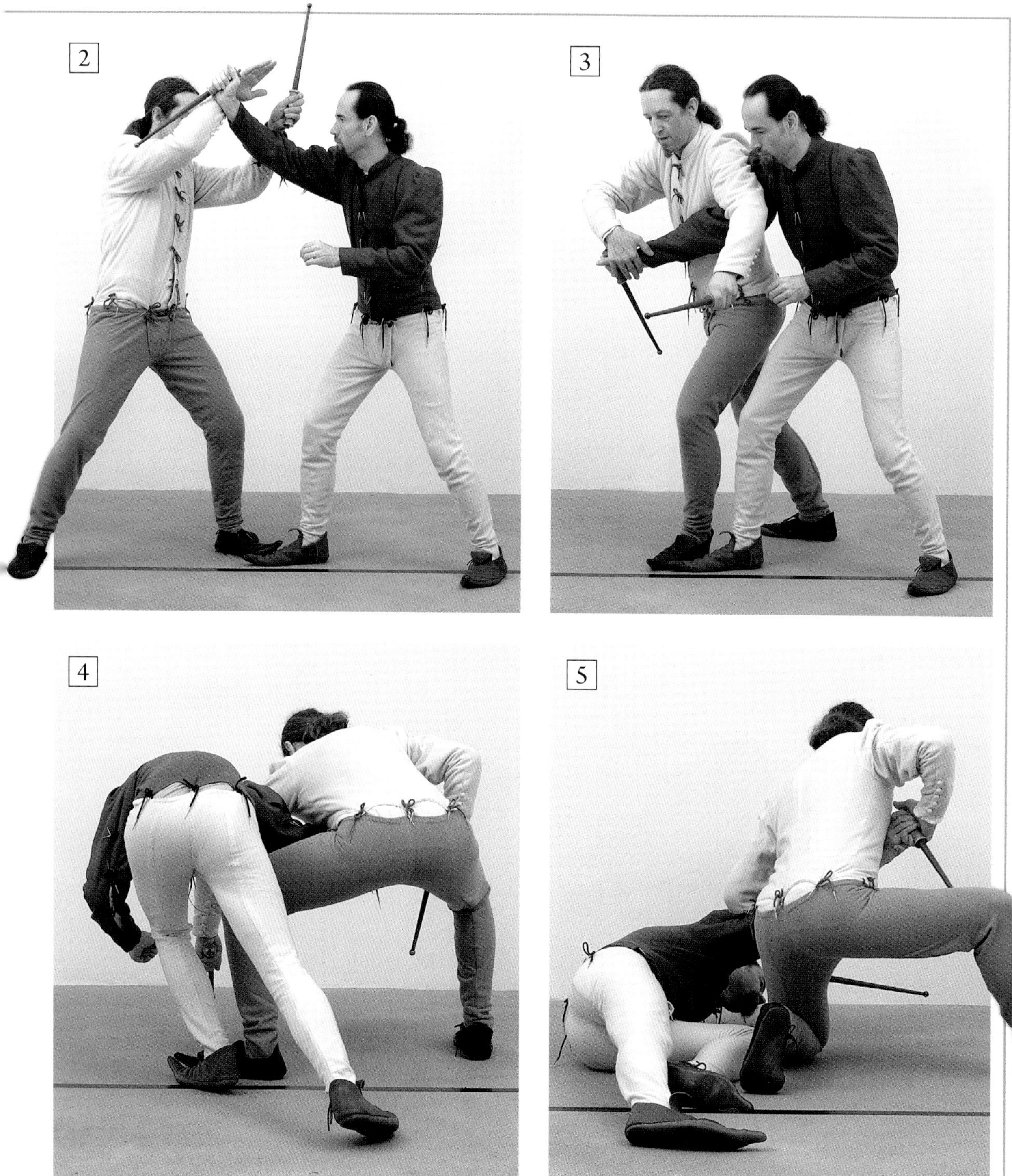
2
3
4
5

DAS NIEDERWÜRGEN (The Choke-Down)

1 Clemens begins with a stab from the From the Roof Guard. Ralf is in the Free Guard.

2 Clemens stabs downward and, as Ralf is very close, he threatens to literally overrun him. Ralf therefore steps his left foot out to the left.

3 As he does so, he lets go of the blade with his left hand, builds momentum with his arm and upper body and, reaching over Clemens' weapon arm and right shoulder, grasps him around the neck in order to choke him down (Ralf has to build momentum, as he must push Clemens a little to the left with his body, in order to seize him and thus throw him off balance and break his attacking energy).

4 Ralf squeezes Clemens' arm and neck firmly against his right side.

5 Clemens still tries to grasp his assailant with his right (weapon) arm (the illustration in the Cod. icon. 394a also shows the fighter who has been seized still trying to grip his opponent).

6 7 If Ralf has seized his opponent, he goes to his knees and with his left hand grips Clemens' thigh from behind and outside. Then he stands up, taking Clemens' leg in his grasp with him, and turns clockwise about his own axis. He thus throws Clemens from him.

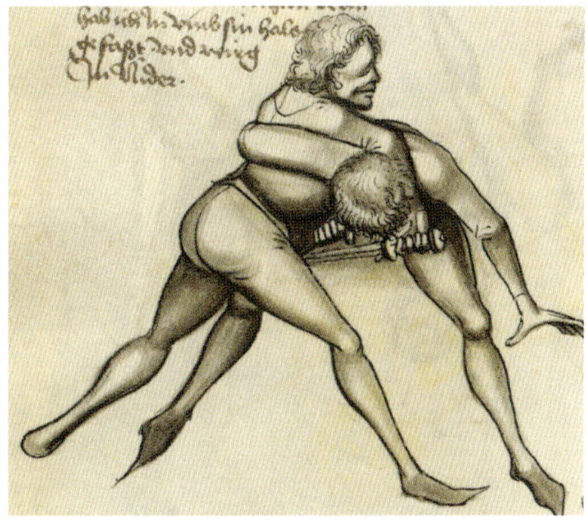

From the Cod. icon. 394a

"Als der mich überloffen hat mit aim fryen stich oben Nyder. So hab ich den lincken arm uff geworffen und versetzt mit mym rechten Arm hab ich In umb sin hals gefaszt und wirg In Nyder"

1

2

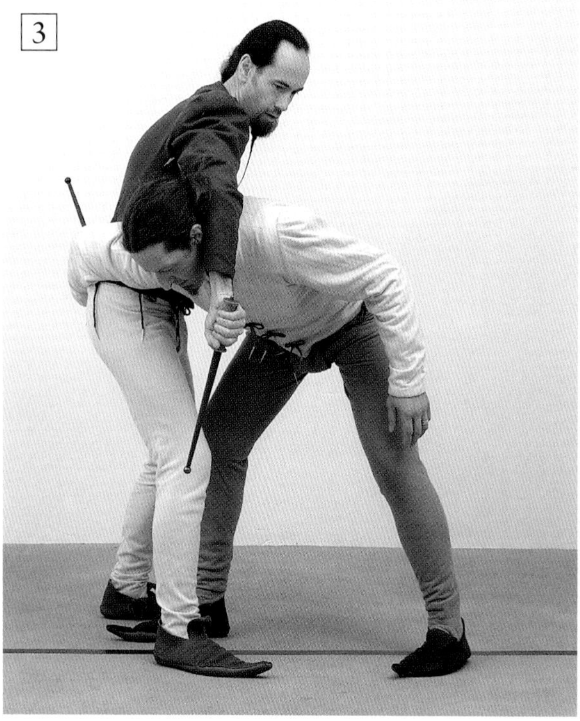
3

4

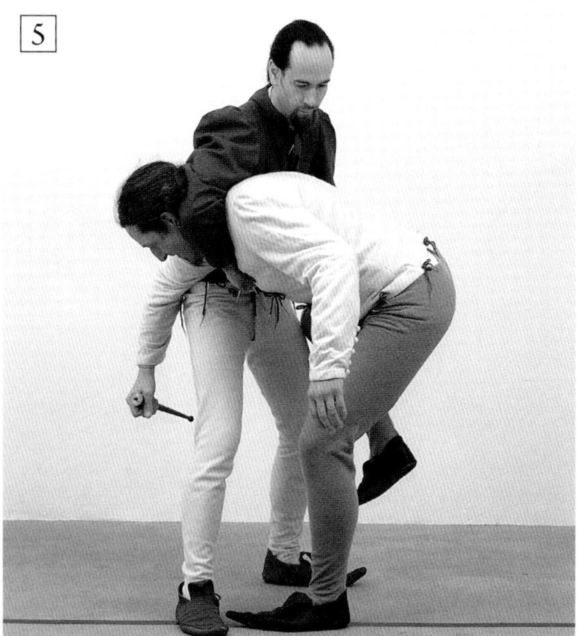
5

6

7

Close-Up

Here is a close-up of Ralf grasping Clemens' thigh.

UM DEN HALS SCHLAGEN
(Strike around the Neck)

From the Cod. icon. 394a

"Aber für den obern stich fach sin stich uff din Rechten Arm und Tryt für und schlah Imi din lincken arm an sin halsz und würff In über die huffen"

1

1 Ralf attacks Clemens with a descending stab from the From the Roof Guard.

2 As soon as the stab comes, Clemens, who is in the Free Guard, explicitly goes forward left to get to Ralf's right side. As he does so, Clemens raises his dagger arm and blocks the stab with his forearm against Ralf's.

3 As soon as Ralf's stab is blocked, Clemens brings his dagger under Ralf's weapon arm, specifically under the wrist on its inner side.

4 While doing so, Clemens aims the tip of his blade at Ralf's face. The entire time he maintains contact with Ralf's weapon arm with his weapon arm (so that he can feel Ralf beginning a movement with his weapon arm and react immediately). Meanwhile Clemens steps his left foot further behind Ralf, from behind places his left hand on Ralf's left shoulder and grasps it.

5 6 7 Subsequently he goes further back and downwards. He pulls Ralf down with him by the shoulder. Because of the threat posed by the blade tip, Ralf does not try to resist Clemens' pull and come forward again.

2

3

4

5

6

7

ÜBER- UND UNTERGREIFEN (Over- and Under-Grip)

From the Cod. icon. 394a

"So hatt der versetzt mit sinen lincken arm und hatt In obern übergryffen und hatt Im under Sinen schenkel undergryffen und wirt In werffen"

1 Clemens is about to make a stab from the From the Roof Guard. Ralf is waiting in the Free Guard.

2 When the stab comes, Ralf blocks it from the inside with his left forearm while stepping out to the left and forward. The attacking arm is not knocked away, however, only stopped. When the arm is stopped, Ralf immediately slides his left arm over that of the attacker.

3 He brings the crook of his arm into Clemens', so that Ralf' arm is pointing straight towards the ground. Then Ralf goes to his knees, which pulls Clemens down with him and keeps his weapon arm bent.

4 On reaching the low point, Ralf moves the wrist of his weapon arm into the hollow of Clemens' right knee and stands up. In the process he pulls Clemens' elbow up towards him with his left arm.

5 6 With his right arm he pulls Clemens' leg, which is in his grip, upwards with him and turns slightly to the left from his hips. He thus throws Clemens behind him.

1
2
3
4
5
6

DAS ENDSTÜCK (The End Play)

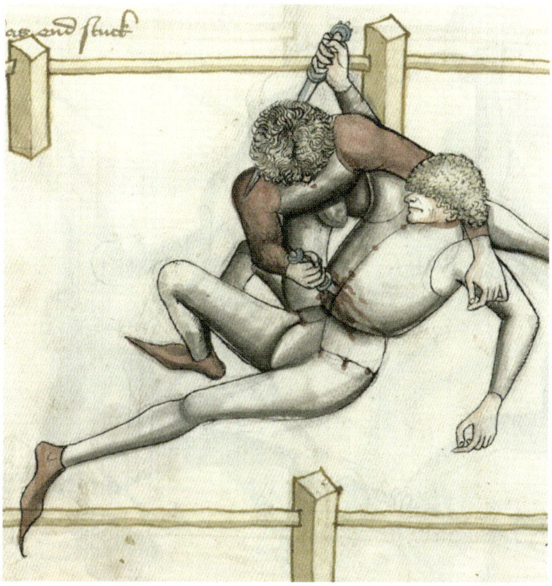

From the Thott 290 2°

"Das end stuck"

1 Ralf makes a stab from the From the Roof Guard.

2 When the stab from above comes, Clemens, who is also coming from the From the Roof Guard, steps his right leg toward Ralf. As he does so he powerfully blocks the attacking arm with his free left hand. One should not knock the hand away, however, instead merely stopping it and creating a little space.

3 Immediately afterwards Clemens steps his left foot close past Ralf on his right side. Clemens' left hand slides along Ralf's arm behind Ralf's neck to his left shoulder. Simultaneously Clemens turns clockwise with his back to Ralf's weapon arm and with his back pushes him backward.

4 Clemens does not stop here, however, instead he continues backward, constantly pushing Ralf's weapon arm backwards with his left shoulder and exerting pressure on Ralf's shoulder with his left hand.

5 6 7 Finally Clemens goes to his knees behind Ralf and pulls him down with him by the shoulder.

In order to prevent Ralf from turning his dagger against Clemens, it is important that Clemens constantly and unrelentingly pushes Ralf's arm backwards with his back. Both cover a considerable distance in the process. We used almost the entire area of the photo studio for this technique, rather more than six meters.

In any case the defender must not stop pushing backwards. As soon as the pressure on the attacker's arm eases, he will stab with his dagger.

2
3
4
5

6

7

DEN DOLCH NEHMEN (Take the Dagger)

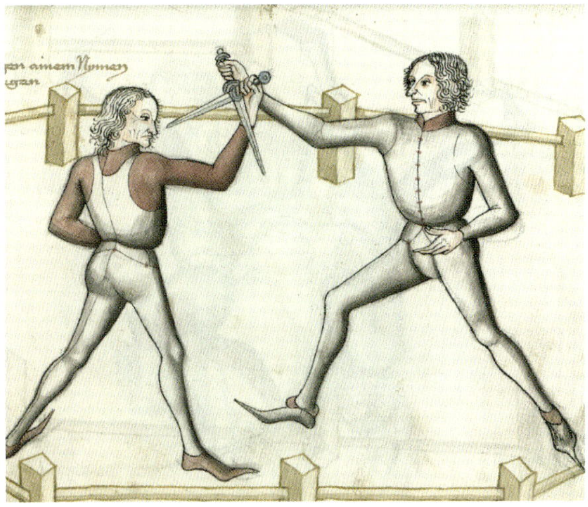

From the Thott 290 2°

"Den tegen ainen Nymen mit sim tegen"

1

1 Clemens approaches from the From the Roof Guard and stabs downward. Ralf, who is also in the From the Roof Guard, awaits the attack.

2 When the stab comes, Ralf parries it from the outside with his blade. As he does this, he takes a step with his right foot forward and to the right, pushing the attacker's blade to the right with him. In this way Ralf creates a gap between Clemens' wrist and his dagger.

3 Ralf then immediately pushes his blade into this gap and places it on the outside of Clemens' forearm.

4 When Ralf's blade is on Clemens' forearm, he lifts the grip of his dagger and thus pushes Clemens' dagger towards and over his forearm.

5 6 To do this Ralf uses his dagger like a lever, that he simply turns. This forces Clemens to let go of his dagger. Ralf's free hand moves to Clemens' weapon hand to secure it.

On the right a close-up of the lever: Ralf parries Clemens' blade with his own. He pushes his blade into the gap between the blade and Clemens' forearm, in order to put it on the outside of the forearm and then lever outward with the grip over Clemens' forearm. He thus uses his dagger to lever Clemens' weapon from his hand.

Another entry to this technique that we like very much is shown in the Codex Wallerstein1: to parry the stab from the From the Roof Guard, the blade of our dagger is placed on the forearm of the weapon hand and the stab is intercepted by it. From there the tip of the dagger is pushed between the opponent's dagger and wrist and placed over his forearm. Thereafter the technique follows the pattern described above. This way of taking a stab from above on the dagger, that is resting on one's own forearm, is used frequently by Master Meyer and in the Codex Wallerstein.

2

3

4

[1]University Library Augsburg: Codex Wallerstein or Baumann's Fencing Manual.

5

6

Close-Ups

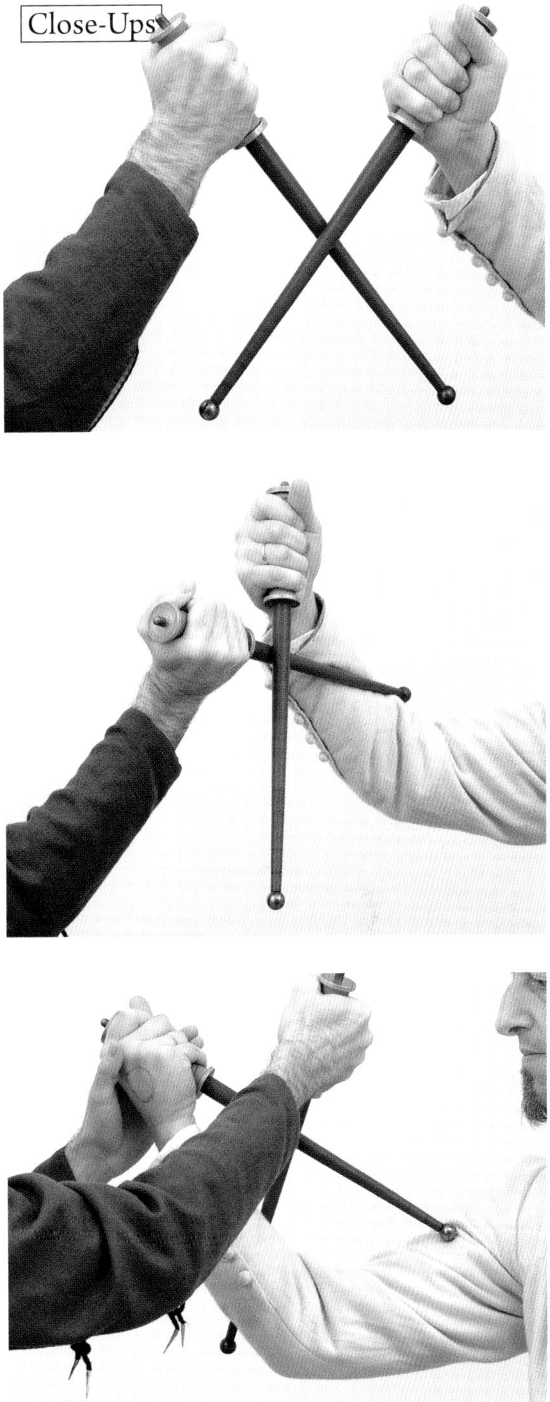

PUNT WIDER PUNT (Punt against Punt)

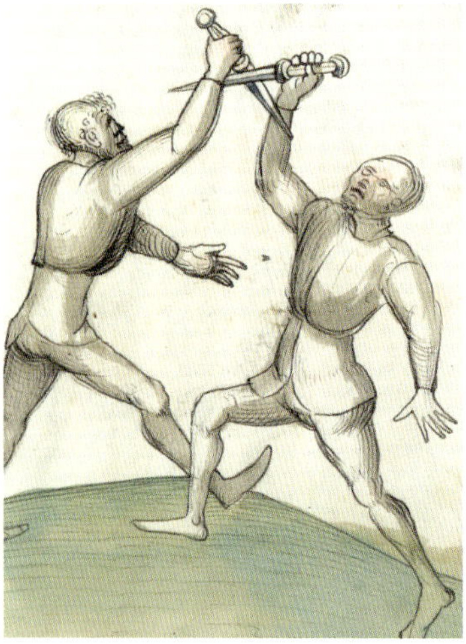

From the KK 5342

"Punt wider punt und den tegen nemen"

1 Both are standing in the From the Roof Guard.

2 When Ralf begins a stab from above, Clemens immediately charges towards him. He moves forward and left, out of line, but just barely.

3 In the process Clemens stabs over Ralf's dagger between his dagger and hand.

4 Then he steps close past Ralf's right side, forcefully continuing his thrust. The stab is aimed behind Ralf's shoulder and simply takes his weapon arm with it in that direction. This creates a very uncomfortable lever against Ralf's shoulder.

5 6 Ralf must yield to this lever, which throws him backward.

According to the Middle High German Dictionary,[2] which is available online, *Punt wider Punt* means "a charge with the war horse when the rider seeks to fall upon the opponent and throw him." This reflects well the character of this technique.

1

2

3

[2] http://germazope.uni-trier.de/Projects/WBB/woerterbuecher/woerterbuecher/bmz/wbgui

4

5

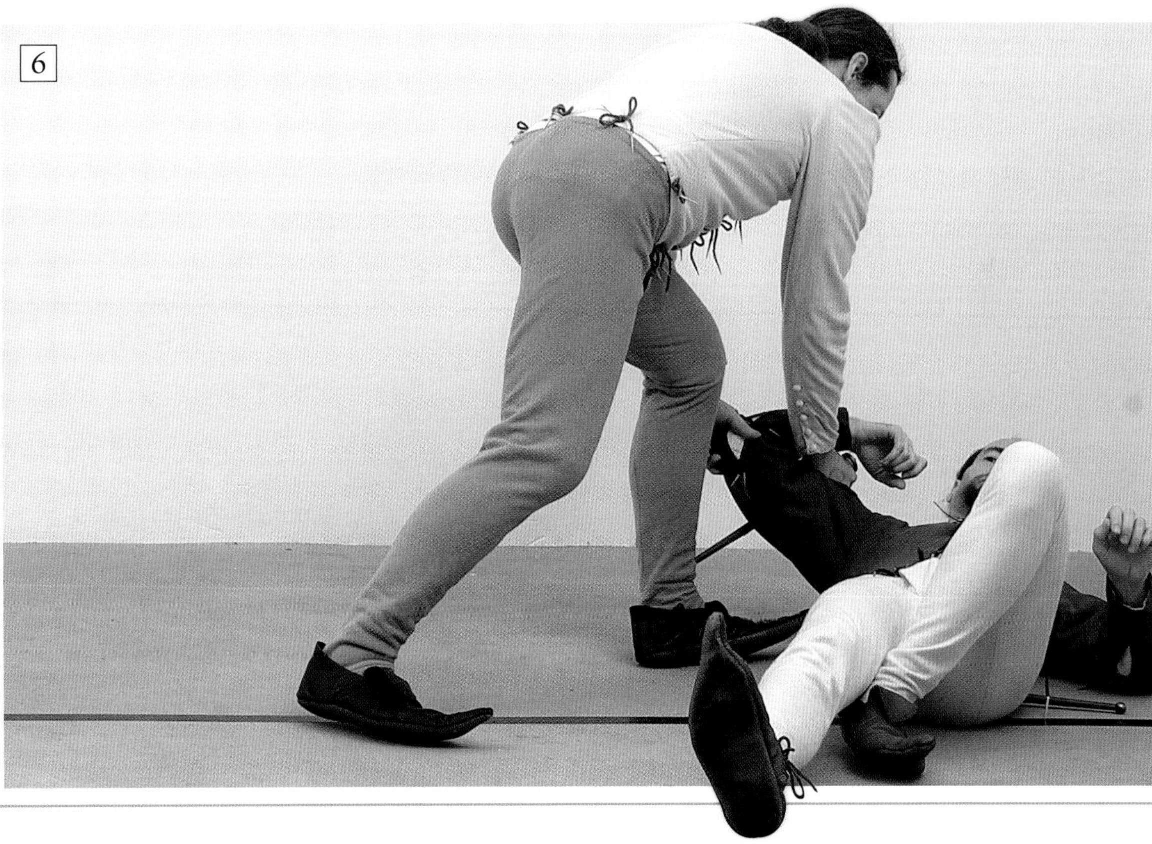

6

DEN DOLCH ERGREIFEN (Seize the Dagger)

From the Ms. Chart. A 558

1 Clemens has assumed the From the Roof Guard, Ralf the Free Guard.

2 When Clemens makes his attack in the form of a descending stab, Ralf takes a step toward the attacker with his left foot. He raises his dagger into the Shield to block the stab on the top end of the blade.

3 If the stab is halted, Ralf lets go of his blade with his left hand and seizes the opponent's blade from above near the grip.

4 When Ralf has seized Clemens' dagger, he moves his own dagger to his left side, in order to exert pressure to the right on Clemens' dagger. The whole time stays hard on Clemens' dagger with his own.

5 Ralf now pulls Clemens' dagger downwards on his own right side. Ralf supports this movement by pushing his blade, which is against Clemens' blade, in the same direction and also turning right at the hips. This wrests Clemens' dagger from him.

4

5

MIT BEIDEN HÄNDEN (With Both Hands)

From the Ms. Chart. A 558

1

1 Ralf begins with an attack from the From the Roof Guard; Clemens awaits him in the Ebich.

2 When the stab from above comes, Clemens moves left and forward and blocks Ralf's stab by stabbing against it frontally/laterally. Forearm strikes forearm, and Clemens stabs over Ralf's arm.

3 When the attack has been stopped, Clemens reaches his left hand through the crook of Ralf's arm in the direction of his own arm.

4 He then steps past Ralf with his right foot while reaching for his right forearm with his left hand.

5 While moving his right foot and reaching through, Clemens continues to push Ralf's arm backwards.

6 7 If Ralf's weapon hand is then behind his back, Clemens changes the direction of pressure from forwards to downwards. Clemens lends support to this by bending forward slightly, giving the movement more emphasis. Ralf has nothing with which to resist the force of Clemens' arms and his body weight and goes backward to the ground.

2

3

4

5

6

7

DAS VERKEHRT WERFEN, VARIATION (The Wrong Way Round Throw, Variation)

1 Clemens attacks with a stab from the From the Roof Guard. Ralf awaits the attack in the Ebich.

2 When Clemens comes down at Ralf with the stab, the latter takes a small step out to the left with his left foot. At the same time Ralf blocks the attacking arm with his weapon hand. In this block Ralf holds his dagger on his forearm and brings it between his and the attacking forearms.

3 As soon as the attack is halted, Ralf reaches for Clemens' wrist with his dagger hand. Ralf is now holding both his dagger and Clemens' wrist in his right hand. He must hurry now, for he cannot control Clemens for long in this way. Ralf therefore turns Clemens' wrist away from him and grips behind his elbow with his left hand.

4 From below he pushes it upwards while stepping his left foot in front of Clemens's right leg. Here too he changes the direction of pressure. At first the pressure on Clemens' elbow is from below. When he steps his left foot forward, he changes the direction of pressure to forward and finally at the end of the technique, combined with a subsequent step with the right foot, to downward.

It is almost the same as rowing: one pushes the oar down and away in order to then pull it up to one's chest and then push it away again. And all of this is in a circular movement.

5 At the end of the technique, when Ralf has pushed Clemens' elbow downward, Ralf bends forward from the hips to put himself into the technique. Once Ralf grips Clemens' elbow with his left hand, he pushes forward constantly, thus exerting pressure with his body.

From the Ms. Chart. A 558

1

2

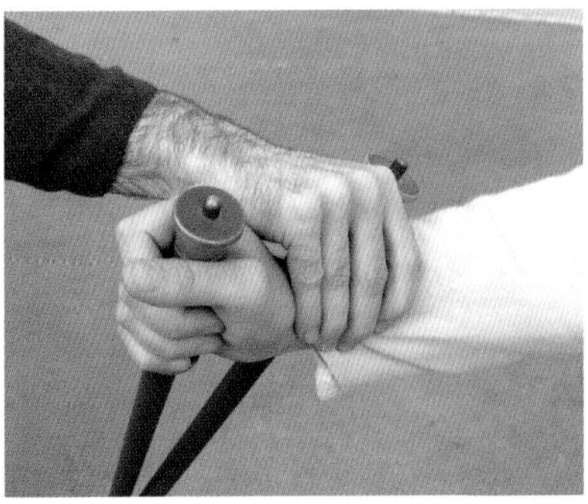

A close-up of the grip on Clemens' wrist. Ralf is holding his dagger and Clemens' wrist in his right hand.

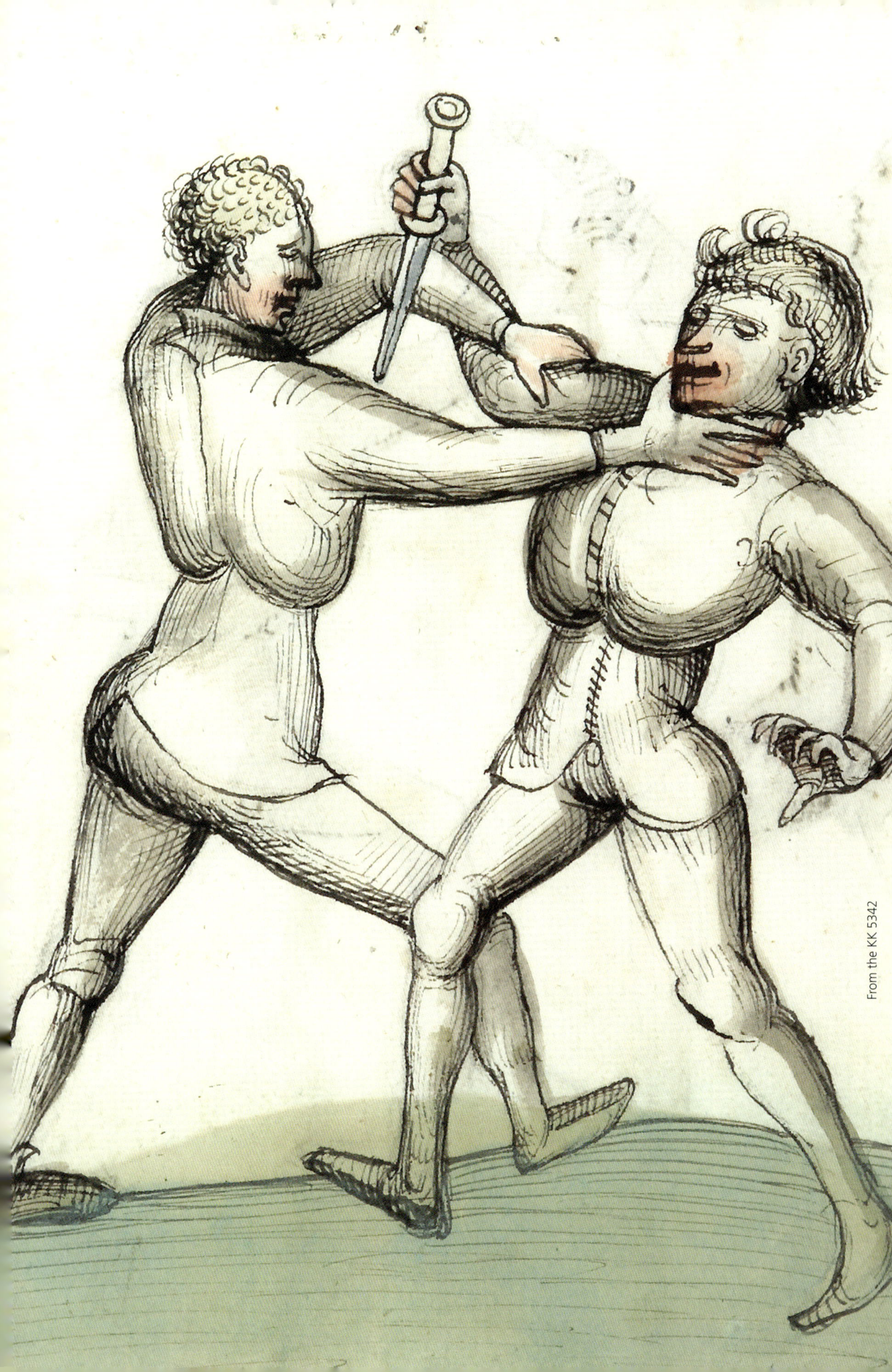

From the KK 5342

Chapter 8: General Tactics

We have already opened up a good part of a fighting system once we know its techniques. What is needed to round out the whole are the principles or the tactical approach that should guide us through this dagger combat. These principles allow us to react instinctively in unexpected situations—provided we have first internalized them. An example is the oft-quoted saying "offence is the best defense," or as Master Ott tells us of wrestling or grappling:

In all wrestling there should be three things.
The first is skill
another is speed
The third is the proper application of strength
Thus you should note that the best is
quickness which does not allow one to use a counter
Next you should note
that with every weaker [person] one should wrestle before
and with every equal one should wrestle with
and with every stronger [person] one should wrestle after
and in all wrestling before works the quickness
In all wrestling with works the scale
and in all wrestling after works the bending of the knee.

One should also take Master Ott's instructions calmly to heart in fighting with the dagger, for in the Late Middle Ages wrestling and dagger fighting were very similar. Not for nothing is fighting with the dagger also called "grappling at the dagger."

Now one can of course try, by reading such general instructions, to derive tactics from the set-plays. Fortunately for us, however, we can find this information in the manuscripts, scattered among the individual dagger chapters. We do not, however, find them in the writings of a single fencing master, rather they are scattered among the writings of several authors. One should therefore tackle as many sources as possible in order to be able to combine the various pieces of information into a complete picture.

It is advisable to look at the originals when possible and not to rely on transcriptions. Fortunately, that is becoming ever easier, because the number of digitized manuscripts available in the internet is growing steadily. Of course working with the manuscripts is very difficult at first. Simply deciphering the *bastarde* seems almost impossible at the beginning, but the vernacular of the time also seems foreign at first. In any case one should not base one's dagger career on the manuscripts at the very beginning, so as not to become overwhelmed. It is worth undertaking, however, if one has been involved in dagger fighting for some time.

In the following we will delve into the principles as found in the manuscripts of Hans Talhoffer, Joachim Meyer and Paulus Hector Mair.

8.1 Master Talhoffer

Although Master Talhoffer is not exactly lavish with words, he does offer a few tips.

The illustration below shows an opponent being blinded by having a hat thrown in his face. Immediately afterwards the dagger is thrown into his chest. This is a suggestion that it is useful to distract the opponent in order to be able to attack him successfully, whether by throwing hats, coins or other odds and ends, a kick in the shin, spitting or anything else that comes to mind.

Two other illustrations from the Ms. Chart A558, which unfortunately have no accompanying text, contain further clues: in one, one sees a man standing in the From the Roof Guard and in front of him another who is falling to the ground. As he falls, the former sticks out one of legs at the standing person, which we interpret as a kick. This is an indication that we are not defenseless, even when falling. From the perspective of the other fighter, the falling man, who probably has as good as lost the fight, is still dangerous. Even while falling he can stab the opponent with his dagger, stick his finger in his eye, kick him or strike him.

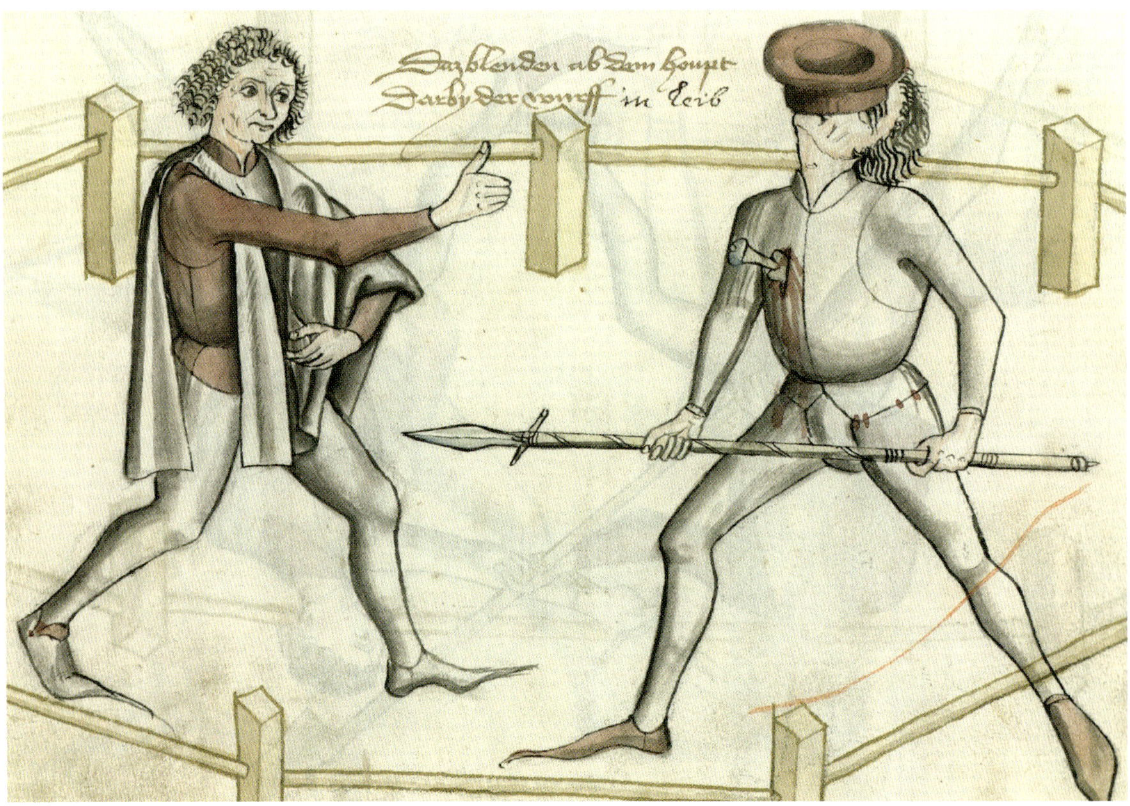

From the Thott 290 2°

The second illustration follows well. In it, one of the two combatants is standing, heedlessly one could say, before the second, who is lying on the ground. The man lying on the ground is sticking his dagger into the thigh of the standing fighter. To our understanding this is an admonishment to always keep an eye on the opponent and to be on guard before an attack—even if he appears to already be defeated.

If we summarize this, Master Talhoffer is giving us the following pieces of advice:

When you attack your opponent or defend yourself, distract him, don't reveal to him what you have in mind and divert his attention to something else. Every resulting fraction of a second that he hesitates, freezes or does not see gives us the advantage.

If the opponent is ever vigilant, always see in him a threat, even if you believe that you have already won. Never be too sure of your position and never underestimate your opponent!

8.2 Joachim Meyer

Published in 1570, Joachim Meyer's work *Thorough Description of the Knightly and Noble Art of Fencing* is a fantastic source for dagger fighting. Meyer is also the most communicative fencing master with respect to information about the techniques.

The body position shown in Master Meyer's illustrations and described in the explanations is as follows: in general the right foot should be forward for a right-hander (especially if we want to attack, which more or less requires us to be in the Before) and the stance shoulder-wide. The upper body should be relatively parallel to that of the opponent, so that the free hand is also forward. The point of the dagger is always aimed at the opponent's face, while the second hand should also be forward but somewhat behind the dagger.

We should bend the knees somewhat and make the body rather smaller in order to build up a significant initial tension. One can thus spring forward quickly when an opening appears. In addition, the back foot should not be all that far behind the front one—at least outside the measure. When we are close to the opponent the stance should be rather wider and this more stable. The rest of the posture is dependent on the respective guard. If, as a right-hander, we have the right foot forward during an attack, our attack will be much faster. The opponent thus has much less time to react to the attack.

Meyer's texts reveal that when attacking, one should never limit oneself to a single attack. Instead one should attack until the opponent is rendered unable to fight. Stabs are often begun with blows with the grip, to paralyze the opponent for a brief instant. One then stabs smoothly from the same movement.

If we decide to make an attack, then we should also carry it out thoroughly. One should not immediately pull back just because the first stab does not find the mark, rather one should immediately fight to the next opening. One does this in the shortest way, not with large circular movements or by withdrawing and the stabbing with the arms. It should come from the elbows, for speed is decisive here.

One can even almost assume that the first stab will be parried and that one must attack the next opening. One should therefore not commit the mistake of making the first attack only halfheartedly. Every attack must be made with emphasis, even if it is a feint.

We take what we can get, preferably without exposing ourselves to excessive danger. Initially the opponent's hands are the easiest target to reach. If his hands or arms are wounded by stabs or cuts, the opponent becomes slower, less controlled, perhaps panicky, furious or even unable to fight. Meyer therefore advises that one attack the opponent's hands and arms whenever the opportunity presents itself. And if the opponent is then struck, it is time to follow up!

But even purely for defense, the hands are a worthwhile target: if the opponent attacks and one is unable or does not want to get close enough to employ a technique or stab at the body, one can also try to keep him at bay by stabbing at his hands. If he attacks, one can retreat and stab at the attacking arm.

Much can happen between the time we prepare to begin a stab at the opponent and the moment when the blade enters his body (if the technique works). The opponent will fight back instead of allowing himself to be killed so easily. When attacking, therefore, one should always move the free hand forward. This enables one to support one's attack or react more quickly to an unexpected action by the opponent and foil it as soon as possible after it is begun.

The second hand should always accompany the weapon hand, even in defense, in order to support it or to be able to react quickly (as far away from one's body as possible) to something unexpected. The free hand should never overtake one's dagger, however, instead it should always be a little behind it. Otherwise you can easily become the target!

If we have gripped the dagger short, no matter in which guard, we should always try to stab over the opponent's attack, especially if our right foot and therefore our weapon hand are forward. This enables us to grasp the opponent's arm, pull it down and throw him off balance. Once we have pulled him down, we should immediately attack with a blow with the handle or a stab.

A blow with the dagger handle is usually followed immediately by a stab. This is done in such a way that the blow from the dagger handle with the dagger held short is made upwards, at the chin for example. The handle blow is continued until the weapon hand is over the opponent's head, in order to immediately make a downward stab. There should be no break between the up and down movements. Both should be executed in a flowing movement.

If one strikes the opponent with the hand not holding the weapon, one should not be satisfied with that, instead always immediately thrusting the dagger at the next opening. For the opponent will not delay long, instead he will immediately continue his attacks, whether with the dagger or—if we have taken it—by hitting, kicking or other nastiness.

8.3 Paulus Hector Mair

Paulus Hector Mair wrote several works, which at least as far as illustrations are concerned are among the most beautiful pieces. The following information is from the Mscr. Dresd. C 9a.

The description of the fencing process and its naming is very interesting. Mair calls the approach *Zufechten* and the establishment of contact as *Bindung* (binding) or *Anbinden* (tying). It is clear today that the individual segments of the combat are called thus, but Mair was probably the first to use them with dagger fighting.

Where footwork is concerned, Mair carries out attacks with both the right and left foot forward, with attacks predominating in which the right foot leads. Some of Master Mair's set-plays seem overloaded with technique sequences. There is speculation that these were purely training pieces that were intended to offer a variety of possibilities. Where some set-plays are concerned, it is entirely possible that one cannot implement the entire sequence of techniques, however parts are sufficient to end a combat victoriously.

Mair advises that when one initiates a stab, one should not reach back or twitch with the weapon hand. The stab should shoot from the resting position, which the guard more or less offers, straight into the target. As well, the feet should not "patter" before one begins to move. The opponent will observe that and thus see the attack coming before one really begins to move.

When stabbing at the opponent, the elbows should not be completely extended when the stab strikes. Not until the moment of contact should the arms be almost straightened. This gives the stab more emphasis. A stab delivered in this way may even make it possible to sweep a halfhearted displacement aside and reach the target.

Mair recommends placing the left foot forward and laying the left hand on the chest when approaching the opponent. In this position one is supposed to observe how the opponent is holding the dagger in order to estimate which type of thrust poses a threat: if he grips his dagger short, the threat is a stab from above. If he is gripping the dagger short but is holding his hand in front of his chest as he steps forward, he intends to deliver a middle thrust. If he is holding the dagger long, the threat is a thrust from below.

In several set-plays Mair recommends approaching the opponent with thrusts and blows, in order to get to the man. That means we should constantly occupy the opponent with thrusts and blows as we near him. One should, however, proceed very deliberately when delivering blows, so that the hands do not become a target. Actually one can only deliver a blow at the moment when the opponent's dagger is otherwise engaged.

8.4 Summary

If we summarize the suggestions from the various writings we get something like what you see here:

First we should always be watchful to keep our eye on the opponent and never underestimate him. One should also pay attention to one's surroundings, so that one is aware of obstacles over which one could stumble, to other possible attackers or spatial conditions that one might be able to exploit. One must also not make the mistake of carelessly regarding the other as beaten, for even an apparently beaten opponent can still be dangerous.

Conversely this also means that one should not give up if one is in a bad position. Even when falling, one can still stab, kick and punch. And sometimes when one is caught in a lever, it may be better to allow one's arm be broken than to lose one's life. That is, of course, just a theoretical consideration.

When one is standing in front of the opponent, one's dagger should always pose a threat with the point aimed at him. In keeping with the precept of the Before, one should seize the initiative and attack the opponent. In doing so, it can always be helpful to distract the opponent during the attack—whether by throwing something into his face, by suggesting the intention of doing something else through a body movement, or whatever comes into one's head at the moment. The possibilities are many and varied.

One must be careful not to signal the coming attack to the opponent, for example by twitching the dagger hand before the stab is made or moving the feet before taking the step. The dagger, like the feet, must spring forward from a resting position.

When one decides to attack, one should do it resolutely and not hesitate. One should not retreat if the first thrust does not strike the target, instead one should change through and stab at the next opening, repeating this until an opening is reached. If one "has" the opponent, continue pressuring him and do not let him go. As long as he is forced to defend himself, it is difficult for him to attack.

Both in the attack and the defense, the free hand should always follow the dagger hand. Thus one can respond quickly to counterattacks, support one's dagger hand if necessary or more quickly execute levers.

One always selects the opponent's face as the first target. Many fencers instinctively do the wrong thing when their face is threatened: they turn away. Good for the other!

If the dagger finds its target, the arm must not be extended when the stab lands. Not until the dagger enters the target should it be fully extended—as if one wants to stab through the target. In this way the stab develops considerably more force. Proper footwork also increases force. The foot on the weapon hand side should touch down at the same moment that the stab lands.

If one parries a stab with the free hand, one must simultaneously stab at the opponent's nearest opening with the dagger. Should our dagger attack be stopped for some reason and we cannot immediately change through with stabs, we attack the opponent with punches, kicks, blows to the head or similar measures.

In turn, the arm must not make any counter-movement when changing through in order to reach the next opening. Movement must come from the elbow. That is very quick and difficult for the opponent to parry. One can thus expect the second or third stab to find its target. But the first strike should not represent the end of an attack. Instead one should stab two or three times before withdrawing with the utmost caution.

In combat one should always take every opportunity to deliver pommel blows. In this way one can briefly paralyze the opponent and then deliver a stab. Basically we stab at the first target that presents itself. That is often the opponent's hands and arms.

If one finds oneself in the After, one should always try to stab over the opponent's stabs. In doing so, one pulls his arm downwards in order to put him off balance and create a tempo advantage for oneself. From this position one immediately attacks the opponent with a stab or pommel blow. One should immediately follow a pommel blow with a stab.

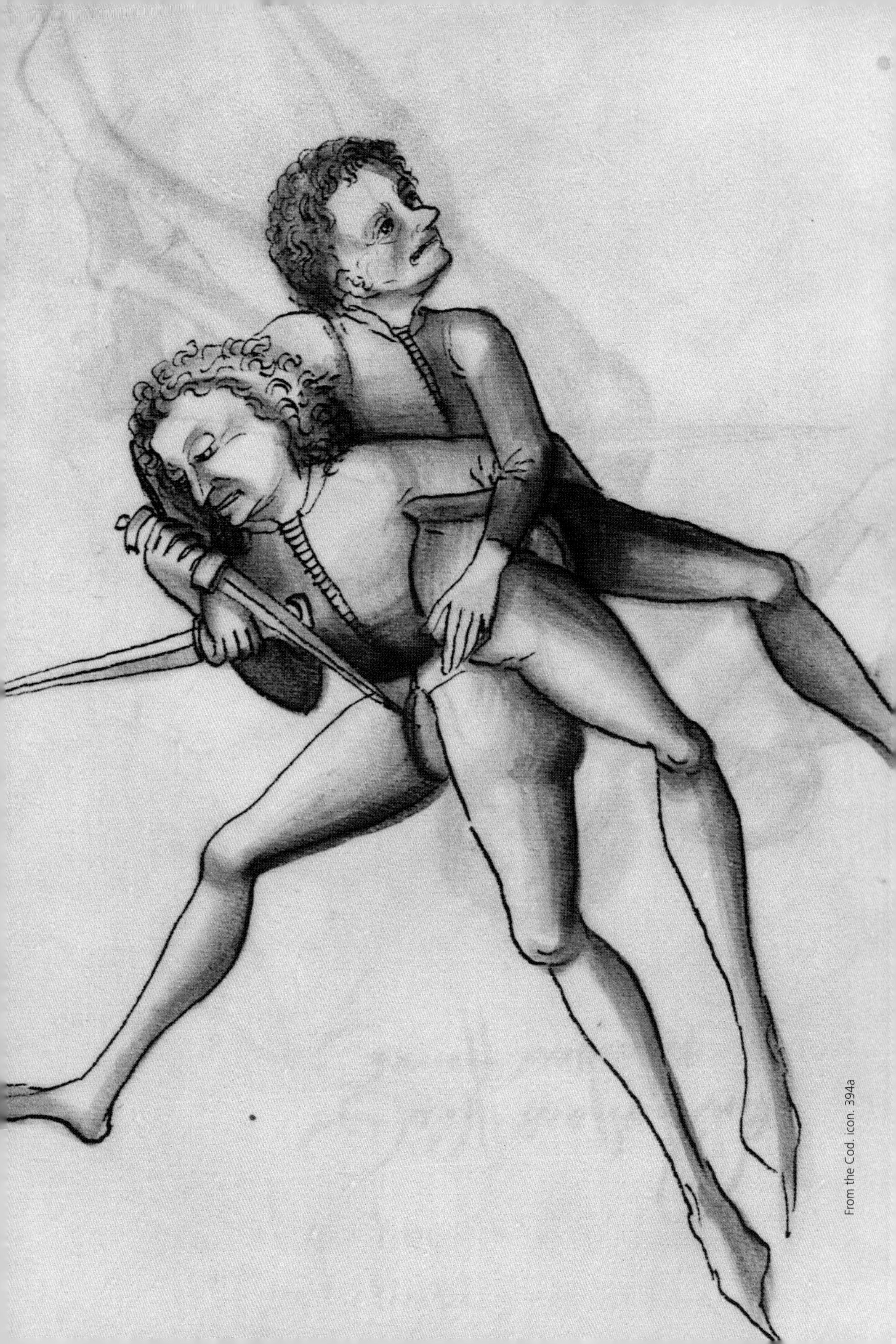

From the Cod. icon. 394a

Chapter 9: Appendices

9.1 Training

When you begin fencing with the dagger, your training should be as structured as possible. Do not simply dive into the thing and begin somewhere, instead follow a plan. Obviously, one should warm up before training, by running, doing sit-ups, push-ups, gymnastics or other exercises. Stretching (once warmed up) is also important in order to avoid injuries and make the body more flexible.

Falling exercises are also recommended. If we wish to carry the techniques through to the end, this often means that one of the two combatants ends up on the ground. This can lead to injuries if the one thrown does not know how to let himself fall.

It is also advisable to improve one's fitness through other sporting activities. Endurance sports such as swimming, running or bicycling are useful, as are weight training and other types of sport.

If one begins working with the set-plays before one knows how to correctly attack and parry, one will quickly become confused. There are simply too many things that one must keep in mind. If you begin fencing before you are sure of the set-plays and techniques, you will never master them properly.

It is important that the individual techniques become a normal reaction during combat. One can only achieve this through repeated practice. If one begins fencing before this happens, habits will develop that are difficult to get rid of later. For in the hectic pace of combat one always tends to do what comes quickly and easily, and that is simply not the complicated techniques, but instead a stab or cut.

If something about the techniques does not work at the outset, try it with less force. One really doesn't need a great deal of force for any of the techniques. Should the techniques not work immediately, go over them again precisely and slowly. Change roles—perhaps the practice partner will see why this is. Or one can leave the technique be at first and turn to other techniques. Perhaps working through other techniques will suddenly make the previously unclear point clearer. If the number of techniques put aside becomes ever greater, perhaps one should become concerned.

Begin slowly and only increase speed gradually, when you are sure and can execute the movements correctly. But above all be sure that your training partner is safe! The speed during training is always determined by the one who is less practiced.

Begin by practicing attacks from the guards and parrying these thrusts. Be sure to make clean thrusts, which are delivered straight and not in a wavy line. Endeavor to stand somewhat lower than normal and to retain this "depth" when taking steps.

Do not work with the arms alone, but with the entire body, and always pay attention to your footwork. This is true both for attacks and displacements. Always try to step slightly to the side when attacking or defending, in order to come at the opponent from the side if possible. Only when that is achieved should you proceed to the next step.

As soon as you begin practicing thrusts more quickly, especially thrusts into the upper area, it is most advisable to wear a fencing mask. Something can always go wrong and an eye can be quickly destroyed!

Once you have mastered the fundamentals, then turn to the set-plays. Go through set-play after set-play until you can execute them all without having to check how they work. Do not ignore the set-plays of which you are not so fond—instead practice them repeatedly until they, too, go smoothly. Of course each has techniques that he is fond of using in combat and employs most often. Nevertheless, one should not deny oneself any possibility in combat.

Whatever you do with the dagger, be careful! Even if you are using a practice weapon it has a point—perhaps a blunt one, but still a point. And this can definitely be dangerous to an eye.

It is clear that at least two are required to effectively practice the set-plays. Three is even better. Mistakes are not always obvious to the one executing a technique, at least as long as they to not hinder the execution of the technique. Sometimes too, one notices a mistake but simply does not know the reason for it. Here a third person watching the situation from the outside is very helpful. A third sees the whole thing and not just an element of it.

Once familiar with the set-plays and able to execute them fluidly, one can turn to combat practice. By this point at the latest it is highly advisable to use gloves, a fencing mask and a protective vest. A fencing mask by itself is only sufficient if one is using a fabric dagger.

Play with everything you have learned, but not yet from combat rather from individual attacks. One combatant takes position, assuming a favorite guard (or none at all) to meet the attack. The other begins his attacks, first ten times from the From the Roof Guard, then ten times from the Zwiffelstich and so on. The number of repetitions and the sequence are irrelevant, but one should choose a number so that each has the same opportunity to practice. If something does not want to work, then devote sufficient time to it until it does.

The defender should now parry the attacks while employing every technique that comes to mind. As one also tends here to only use what seems easy, you should give each other suggestions for additional possibilities. In this way you can expand your abilities together.

If you can now confidently counter every attack without hesitating (of course, now and them something will go wrong, but that is always so…), it is time to approach combat.

Protective clothing is absolutely mandatory. In order to avoid injury, we recommend gloves, a fencing vest or similar, a fencing mask, a neck protector and a lower body protector. Even if the dagger is "only" made of wood, it has enormous penetrative power in a thrust. One should therefore never stab with full power. This can go wrong, even when wearing protective clothing.

One should also be very careful when beginning levers, so as to avoid injury to joints. We recommend that you end the combat when one has the other firmly in a lever. We operate in such a way that the one gripped stops resisting at a certain point. This is not intended to mean that you should not try to escape a lever, but only try it to a certain point and then give that up too. You will quickly discover where that point is during practice.

If you need power when executing a technique, then don't develop it just from the arms, rather from the entire body—by turning the hips or for example by repositioning the back leg in order to turn the opponent around. The power that comes from the entire body is significantly greater than that from the arms alone. If we heed this, it is possible to lever, upset or spin round even a much stronger opponent.

Use the opponent's movements: if he presses towards you, do not push against his chest to force him away from you. Instead select a technique that leads in the direction chosen by him. In this way it is possible to defeat an opponent who is stronger and against whom we could not succeed with pure muscle power.

Now it may be that one cannot choose the direction and must bring the attacker in a certain direction. This may be simply because he is standing like a rock. Then we must put him off balance before we employ the actual technique. For example, by seizing him and pulling on him, forcing him to make a sidestep. Only then can one begin the technique.

Or we must distract him. To do this, we must do something that draws his complete attention for a brief moment. This can be a kick to the inner thigh, a punch in the stomach, a knee, a blow, or a hat thrown in the face, as Master Talhoffer showed us. This makes the opponent more vulnerable to our technique for a moment. But make haste, the moment is fleeting. And the more experienced our opponent, the shorter is this moment.

Do not make the mistake of fencing to the exclusion of all else. Continue working on the attacks, the displacements, the technique training and the set-plays. It is best to split up the training: warm-up, attacks and displacements, the set-plays, technique training. Free fighting. Of course you can distribute the emphasis as you see fit.

And do not forget learning the martial art is a means to an end.

9.2 Protective Gear

Here we would like to introduce the protective gear used by us. You will not need it during the initial slow technique training, but even there a groin and chest protector cannot hurt. When you begin practicing stabs to the face, you should definitely use a fencing mask. One must also use a fencing mask or other protector with really fast thrusts to the body. And when you proceed to free fighting, it is advisable to wear the full suite of protective gear.

Unfortunately these things are not all cheap, but one does not have to buy everything. As one should only practice the techniques in the beginning, one can gradually add equipment until then entering into fencing.

The protective gear described in the following text consists of components that have proved their worth to us. One can of course use other protective gear, either from other sports or homemade items. They fulfill their purpose and protect the wearer.

GLOVES

Lacrosse gloves have proved very effective for use in historical fencing. They are light, have little material on the inside, allowing one to grip well, and as an added feature some models have "scales" over the finger joints, thus protecting the joints even when grasping. Such gloves are available from various online shops.

FENCING MASK

Fencing masks can be found in sporting goods stores. When selecting one, ensure that the mask is marked with (FIE) 1600 N. The "weaker" models will not suffice here. The back of the head should also be protected. The Allstar company distributes a mask for historical fencing which offers protection for the back of the head. As an alternative solution, one can sew a protector for the back of the head oneself.

GROIN PROTECTOR

Not much needs to be said about this. Every man knows why it is better to wear one than not, if one is hit. There are also breast protectors for women, which we recommend. One should also wear groin or breast protection when technique training.

FENCING VEST

The *Fechtmeister* fencing vest offers good protection for the upper body and absorbs most of the force of even powerful thrusts. It is made of suede and has a removable inner lining which protects the entire upper body. Vests can be purchased where fencing supplies are sold. Unfortunately, they are not exactly cheap, as they are usually made to measure.

Good upper body protection: Fechtmeister vest obtainable from supplier soft fencing equipment.

Best with protection for the back of the head: commercially-available fencing mask.

Not designed for fencing, but well-suited for it: lacrosse gloves.

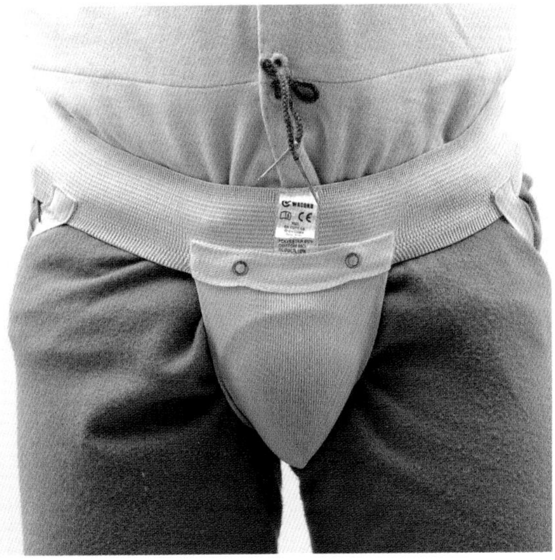

Always recommended: groin protector for sensitive areas.

Actually designed for flying pucks: effective throat protection from street hockey.

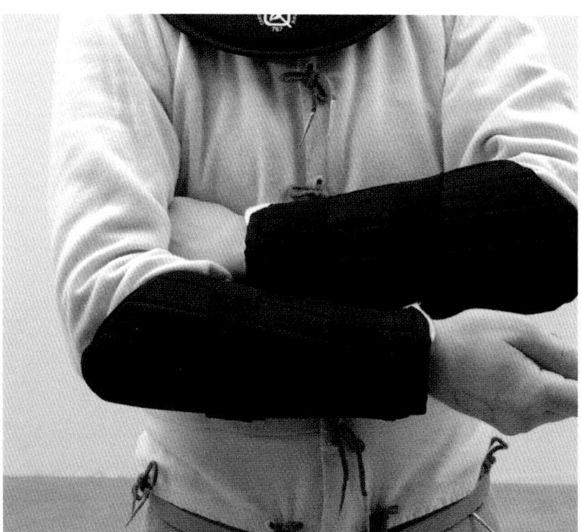

Adopted from Philippine martial arts: eskrima forearm guards.

THROAT PROTECTOR

Even if it is unlikely that a stab will slide under the mask or over the vest's neck guard and strike the throat, if it does happen a throat protector can save life. There is also no reason not to wear one while technique training. One can obtain such a protector where ice or street hockey supplies are sold.

Underarm Protectors

Underarm protectors are quite practical for intensive stabbing and blocking exercises. They can be obtained where eskrima supplies are sold. One should not wear them at all times, rather one should carry out all technique exercises without underarm protection once, in order to accustom the underarms with contact.

9.3 Instructions for Making a Free-Fighting Dagger

It is impossible to really learn the techniques and their functionality without executing them at full speed with emphasis. With a stiff dagger this entails considerable risk of injury— even if protective gear is worn. It is therefore better to use a special dagger that has a lower potential for injury. The same is true of free fighting. As there is no suitable practice dagger on the market, we have made one ourselves.

All the materials and tools needed to produce a practice dagger.

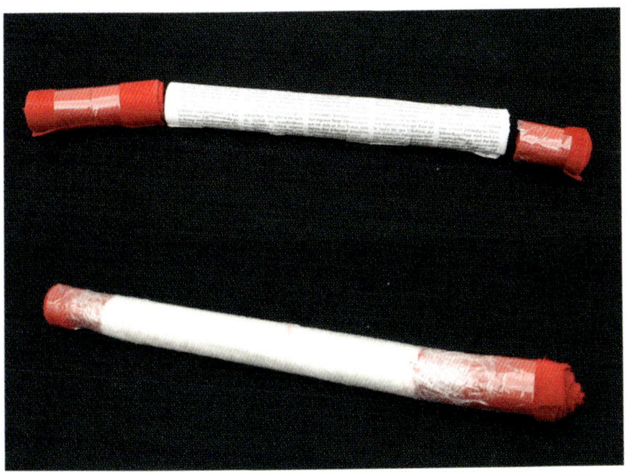

The core of the dagger: in the middle a stiff piece of rolled-up newspaper, at the ends softer rolls of cloth. The whole thing is put together with adhesive tape.

The solution that has proved optimal is a fabric dagger. Even though it sounds a little funny at first, it offers everything we need. Over much of its length it is stiff enough to execute levers. The ends, on the other hand, are so well padded that stabs and pommel blows are strongly cushioned.

At its core, the stiff part consists of a tightly rolled newspaper wrapped with plenty of adhesive tape. The front and back ends consist of rolled cloth. The rolled newspaper and rolled fabric must have the same diameter. The two cloth elements are attached to the newspaper body with adhesive tape. The entire thing is then fitted with a tight covering of cloth.

To make a fabric dagger therefore we need an old newspaper, plenty of wide adhesive tape, sturdy scraps of cloth, needle and thread, a felt marker or similar, a folding ruler and a pair of scissors. Assembly takes an hour at most.

First we must decide how lone we want to make the dagger. If it is too long it will be unstable, if it is too short it will deny us many possibilities. After several attempts an overall length of about 35 centimeters with an approximate diameter of four centimeters proved ideal. Our instructions apply to a fabric dagger with these dimensions. One can adjust the dimensions if desired, however. The two cloth ends should keep their dimensions regardless of the overall length. If one adds width to the cloth components that area becomes too flexible. If one takes away too much width, the area—and thus the impact—becomes too hard.

After we have determined how large the dagger is to be, we must first cut the cloth for the ends and the newspaper to a suitable width. In our case, for the front end we need a strip of cloth about ten centimeters wide, and for the rear end a strip approximately five centimeters wide. The length of the two strips of cloth depends on the desired thickness of the completed dagger and the strength of the fabric used. One should make a test wrap to see how thick the whole thing will be. We cut the newspaper to a width of about 20 centimeters. When

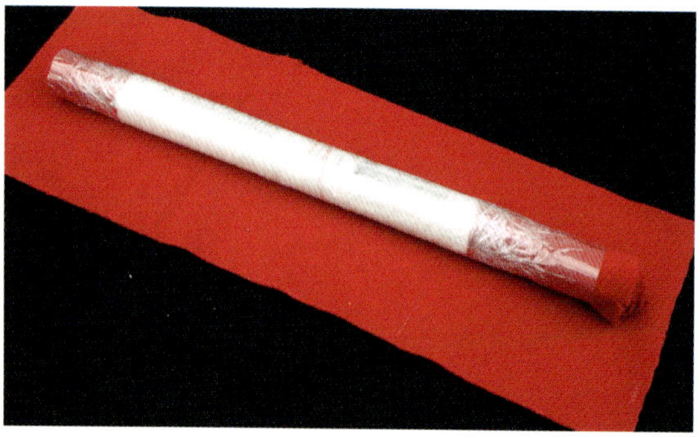

The outer cloth cover is measured and cut out with about a centimeter's extra length and five centimeters width.

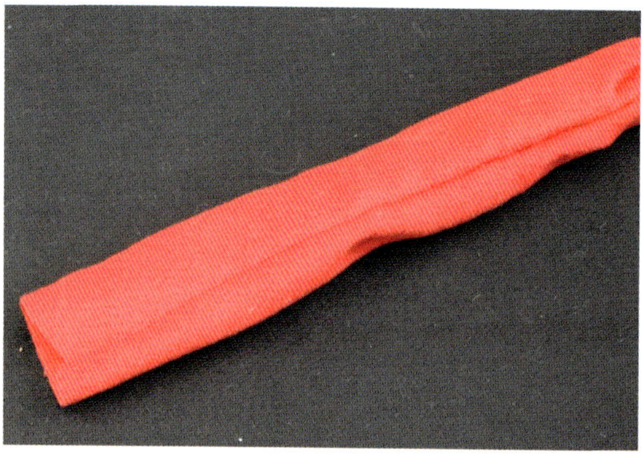

The tube is first sewn together, on the long side and one of the two ends.

Then we insert the core into the cover.

cutting the cloth and the newspaper to length, one must be sure that the three parts will have as close to the same diameter as possible. It is impossible to be precise, but it should be as exact as possible, for otherwise the dagger will be misshapen and unstable.

The newspaper core is rolled up as tightly as possible until it has the desired diameter. Any excess length is cut off. The center of the newspaper roll is then wrapped tightly several times with adhesive tape. For lever techniques, it is really vital that the newspaper core is wrapped really tightly. Otherwise, after a few practices it will in the truest sense of the word buckle. We proceed similarly with the rolled cloth sections, however they are wrapped loosely with adhesive tape rather than tightly. Simply wrapping them with tape is sufficient here. If one uses too much tape, the fabric core will be too rigid.

Now we have a roll of newspaper and two rolls of cloth, which together will form the core of the fabric dagger. The next thing we have to do is connect them. This we achieve with tape. First, each of the two rolls of cloth is attached to the newspaper core with a piece of tape. Here, too, only as much tape as necessary is used, as each layer of tape adds rigidity to the cloth component. One must also be sure that both parts are pressed tightly together. Otherwise a hollow spot can result between the cloth and paper, which negatively affects stability.

When the three pieces have been assembled, take out the tape again and wrap the whole thing generously with several layers. In doing so, we do not wrap all the way to the end of the dagger. Only about a third of the cloth part, adjacent to the newspaper core, is wrapped several times.

Then we can put the dagger core aside and turn to the cloth covering for the core. Measure the length and width of the dagger core, add about ten centimeters for the length of the cloth strip and about five centimeters for the width, and transfer the measurements to the cloth.

Cut out the marked piece of cloth and sew it together at one short and one long side. We sew the whole thing together using the so-called whip stitch. The short side is reinforced with a second seam. The resulting tube is subsequently flipped from left to right, with the aid of a cooking spoon or something similar. When the tube is flipped, we insert the dagger core into it. The front end of the dagger, the side with the wider roll of cloth, is inserted into the tube first. The already sewn short end forms the point of our dagger.

When the dagger core has been inserted into the tube, we sew up the other opening of the tube. One should be sure that the fit of the cover fits tightly over the dagger core. Once the last opening is closed, we again stitch the cover to adjust the width. We gather up as much fabric as possible and using the whip stitch sew it up while maintaining pressure. The free fighting dagger is finished!

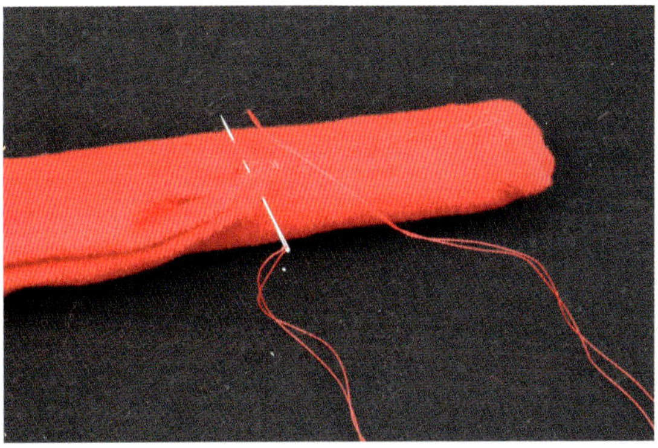

Then the cover is fitted exactly to the core using a so-called whip stitch, so that it sits tightly.

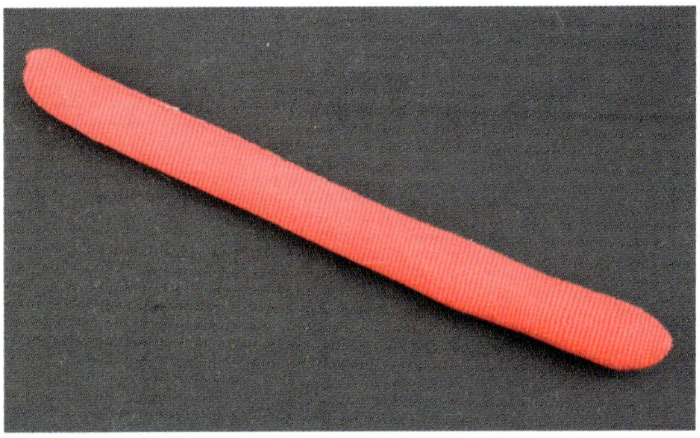

The cover is subsequently turned, the core reinserted and the second end sewed.

9.4 Glossary

Abnehmen
Paulus Hector Mair, for example, characterizes the parrying of a dagger thrust as Abnehmen.

Abziehen/Abzug (Withdraw)
To disengage from the opponent and move out of range of his weapon. Usually after the combat has ended.

Anbinden (Crossing of the Blades)
To place one's blade in contact with that of the opponent, in order to push it out of the way or otherwise control it. One can, however, also bind with the arm, either against the opponent's weapon or his arm.

Angehen (Approach)
This term describes a movement of the dagger before the actual forward movement. It betrays the planned move to the opponent.

Blösse (Openings)
An opening is a gap in the cover. There are four openings: two upper and two lower. The belt line forms the boundary between upper and lower openings. We thus have a left and a right upper opening and a left and a right lower opening.

Bloßfechten
Fencing without armor.

Büffel (Buffalo)
Disparaging term for a fighter who relies solely on his strength and aggression.

Durchwechseln (Changing Through)
To change the side from which one attacks. If one stabs at the opponent from the right and is blocked, one changes through and stabs from the other side, whether it be left, below or above.

Ebich
Reversed or the other way round. Usually refers to the posture.

Fehler (Feint)
A feint. It is carried out as if you are about to attack a certain opening, in order to attack another vulnerable opening.

Indes (Meanwhile)
Not "Before" or "After," but "Meanwhile" or "at the same time." One does something while something else is happening. An example of this is the displacement of a blow by a stabbing blow, which pushes the opponent to the side while (simultaneously) beginning an attack.

Mensur (Measure)
The measure is the distance that two fencers establish between one another. For our purposes we divide it into a wide measure, a medium measure a short measure and a closed measure. In the wide measure neither fencer can reach the other without taking a huge step forward. Dagger fighting is possible in the medium measure, and the opponent's hands and arms can be attacked without having to take a step. In the short measure both fencers can stab the other's body or head or wrestle with the arms without taking a step. In the closed measure we wrestle body to body.

Mittelstich (Middle Stab)
A stab carried out at hip-height.

Nach (After)
One characterizes as "in the After" one of the two fencers who only reacts to the opponent's attacks. He is thus at a disadvantage as he cannot attack, while his opponent will probably strike somewhere if he continues his attacks. One should therefore always try to get into the Before. It is possible, however, to end a combat victoriously from the After. Master Ott even advises the weaker wrestler to wrestle from the After.

Oberstich (Upper Stab)
A downward stab made from above.

Ort (Point)
The tip of the weapon. Some fencing masters are more precise and differentiate between the forward point (the tip of the blade) and the rear point (the pommel of the grip) of daggers.

Reiben (Rub)
Turn to the rear or side.

Ringen (Wrestling or Grappling)
Fighting without weapons, in which levers, throws and also punches and kicks are used. One can switch from fencing to wrestling when the opponent comes very close.

Schwäche/Stärke (Foible/Forte)
In order to explain fencing theory, our ancestors divided the weapon, but also the body, into various zones. Lever techniques can be explained using these divisions. We can see the difference between the foible and forte using a sword: if one is holding the sword in one's hand, the rear half of the blade near the hand is called the forte. The front half of the blade, to the tip, is called the foible. In the forte one has much power and can exert great force. With the foible, on the other hand, it is much more difficult to build up force. In order to push the opponent's blade out of the way, therefore, one must always try to place one's forte against the opponent's foible.

Tempo/Fechttempo (Tempo/Fencing Tempo)
The precise amount of time required to complete an action—a step, a thrust, a displacement or another technique.

Transcription
In our context the conversion of text from the manuscripts into modern writing and also the conversion into modern parlance.

Überlaufen (Overrunning)
This term describes a tactic in which one reacts to an attack on one's legs by stepping back so that the attack can no longer reach one. The opponent's head is simultaneously attacked from above.

Überstechen (Stab Over)
Stab over the attacking weapon arm with one's own dagger in order to parry it. The target is the wrist area of the opponent and the stab is made from above to below. The opponent's arm is caught in the hook formed by one's dagger and forearm. If he is caught, the arm is pulled down and the attacker thrown off balance.

Ubersich
Upwards.

Undersich
Downwards.

Unterbinden (Under-Bind)
Bind from below.

Unterstich (Under-Stab)
A stab made from below. It is usually aimed at the lower openings, but can, for example, be directed at the chin.

Versatz (Displacement)
Blocking of an opponent's attack. Also called parade or block.

Vor (Before)
The fencer who is in the "Before" determines how the fight is conducted. One should therefore always be first to act and this be in the Before.

Winden (Winding)
"Wind around," in order to work around something that is in the way.

Zufechten
Term for a phase of combat in which one approaches the opponent with stabs and possibly cuts, but where there is no contact with the opponent's weapon or body.

Zucken (Drawing)
Stabbing and then immediately stabbing again. The first stab is nothing more than a feint. Usually the first stab is drawn back as soon as the opponent initiates his displacement, in order to this time stab behind the displacement.

9.5 Acknowledgments

Here we would like to thank all those people who helped us, encouraged us or tolerated our passion. As there are two of us, each will have his own say.

Heartfelt thanks to my daughter Denise for allowing me to try out things using a cooking spoon as a dagger simulator, to my son Benjamin who repeatedly impressed me, my wife Michaela, who gave me the time to work on this book, my parents Evi and Peter, who always encouraged my passion, and Ralf, who curiously enough always seemed to share my passion.

Many thanks to Thomas Schwaneke for allowing us to try out techniques with him. It is interesting to try out dagger techniques on a rock.

I would also like to thank Matthias Johannes Bauer, who tirelessly helped me. Not to be forgotten is Hans Joachim Wieland, who made it possible for us to publish this book.

– Clemens Nimscholz

Many thanks to my wife, who with great patience made the necessary time for me to work on this book.

– Ralf Schoetzau

The medieval clothing was made by Anna Lukasiewicz-Tannhäuser.
Contact: www.sew-mill.com

The poulaines were made by Snorri Varnasson.
Contact: www.snorri-varnasson.de

For questions or suggestions, the authors may be reached at their club website: www.twerchhau.de

Der hatt gestochen von dach.
Der hatt versetzt mit ainer hand/vnd hatt den Tegen von im gewandt.